THIS BOOK BELONGS TO

START DATE

SHE READS TRUTH

EXECUTIVE

FOUNDER/CHIEF EXECUTIVE OFFICER
Raechel Myers

CO-FOUNDER/CHIEF CONTENT OFFICER
Amanda Bible Williams

CHIEF OPERATING OFFICER/
CREATIVE DIRECTOR
Ryan Myers

EXECUTIVE ASSISTANT
Catherine Cromer

EDITORIAL

CONTENT DIRECTOR
John Greco, MDiv

MANAGING EDITOR
Jessica Lamb

KIDS READ TRUTH EDITOR
Melanie Rainer, MATS

CONTENT EDITOR
Kara Gause

EDITORIAL ASSISTANT
Ellen Taylor

MARKETING

MARKETING MANAGER
Kayla Stinson

SOCIAL MEDIA STRATEGIST
Ansley Rushing

COMMUNITY SUPPORT SPECIALIST
Margot Williams

CREATIVE

LEAD DESIGNER
Kelsea Allen

ARTIST IN RESIDENCE
Emily Knapp

DESIGNER
Davis DeLisi

JUNIOR DESIGNER
Abbey Benson

SHIPPING & LOGISTICS

LOGISTICS MANAGER
Lauren Gloyne

SHIPPING MANAGER
Sydney Bess

FULFILLMENT COORDINATOR
Katy McKnight

FULFILLMENT SPECIALISTS
Sam Campos
Julia Rogers

SUBSCRIPTION INQUIRIES
orders@shereadstruth.com

CONTRIBUTORS

ARTIST
Christina Moodie (18, 84, 146, 182)

RECIPES
Haylie Abele (67)
Tori DiBartolomeo (203, 231)
Hayden Jordan (151)
Aimee Mars (177)
Emily Maxson (123)
Tynia Peay (93)
Marta Rivera (39)

@SHEREADSTRUTH

Download the
She Reads Truth app,
available for iOS
and Android.

SHEREADSTRUTH.COM

This book was printed offset in Nashville, Tennessee, on 70# Lynx Opaque. Cover is 100# Cougar Opaque with a soft touch lamination.

WOMEN & MEN IN THE WORD

OLD TESTAMENT

God is at work
in every story.

Amanda

Amanda Bible Williams
CO-FOUNDER & CHIEF
CONTENT OFFICER

I was in my thirties the first time I read the story of Tamar from the book of 2 Samuel. It grieved me. It still does. I see the words on the page and want them to come untrue. I want to look away from the injustice.

And yet, Tamar's story moves me to tears for another reason. Present within her grief, within this most tragic part of her story, is her God. We know He is, because the whole of Scripture tells us so.

The Lord is near to the brokenhearted (Ps 34:18), holy and righteous (Lv 19:2; Ps 11:7), compassionate and merciful (Ex 34:6–7). He loves justice (Ps 37:28), and He hates sin (Pr 6:16–19; Ps 11:5). He is all-knowing and all-powerful (1Jn 3:20; Jr 32:17), and He dispels darkness with the light of life (Jn 1:5; 10:10). This is the God who is present in Tamar's story, a story that is itself part of a larger story God is still writing—a story of redemption in which everything will be made new and tragedies like Tamar's will be no more.

This is why we read. This is why, in 2012, a small army of women dared to believe the Bible was for them. And it is! Year after year, that still-growing army opens up Scripture together, and God meets us there, teaching us who He is and who we are in Him. And so we keep reading Truth together, every day.

For the next eight weeks, we will be women in the Word by reading about women and men in the Word—famous and infamous, unknown and well-known, all from the pages of the complete, true, and inspired Word of God. Our study will focus on women and men in the Old Testament, with key questions at the end of each day designed to direct our gaze to God, the hero of every story.

Our team has assembled a beautiful, thoughtful book to guide you through this reading plan. The introductory features, beginning on page 15, provide a biblically sound framework for engaging this diverse group of stories. Don't miss the "Connecting the Stories" extra on page 110, meticulously crafted by our editorial and creative teams to help us understand how the people we read about are connected to one another.

God is at work in every story. May your time spent reading about women and men in the Old Testament draw you into deeper relationship with Him, teaching you to trust and recognize His good hand in these stories and in your own.

DESIGN ON PURPOSE

The line art created for this book serves to highlight key moments in the stories of women and men in the Old Testament. Each subject is drawn only in part, a reminder that what we read in Scripture is but a glimpse into the whole life of each person.

In her *Life Abundant* series, artist Christina Moodie employs vibrant colors and brushstrokes of varying sizes to create her compositions. Her artwork reminds us of the way God tells His story through the lives of unique people.

She Reads Truth is a community of women dedicated to reading the Word of God every day.

The Bible is living and active, breathed out by God, and we confidently hold it higher than anything we can do or say. This book focuses primarily on Scripture, with bonus resources to facilitate deeper engagement with God's Word.

SCRIPTURE READING

Designed for a Monday start, this study book focuses on the stories of more than forty women and men in the Old Testament through daily readings, with supplemental passages for additional context.

RESPONSE

Each weekday closes with questions for reflection and space for response.

GRACE DAY

Use Saturdays to pray, rest, and reflect on what you've read.

WEEKLY TRUTH

Sundays are set aside for weekly Scripture memorization.

Find the corresponding memory cards in the back of this book.

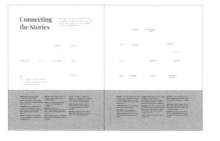

EXTRAS

This book features additional tools to help you gain a deeper understanding of the text.

PLANS

Women & Men in the Word: Old Testament

8 Weeks

PLAN OVERVIEW

As followers of Christ, we are to be women and men of the Word, people who open up our Bibles to meet with God and learn more about Him and His great love for us. And when we read, we find men and women who are, in many ways, a lot like us. Some walked in faith, some stumbled in darkness. Some were used powerfully by God over long seasons, and others had smaller parts to play in the story of redemption. But every one is important, because God saw fit to include them in His Word.

Table of Contents

30

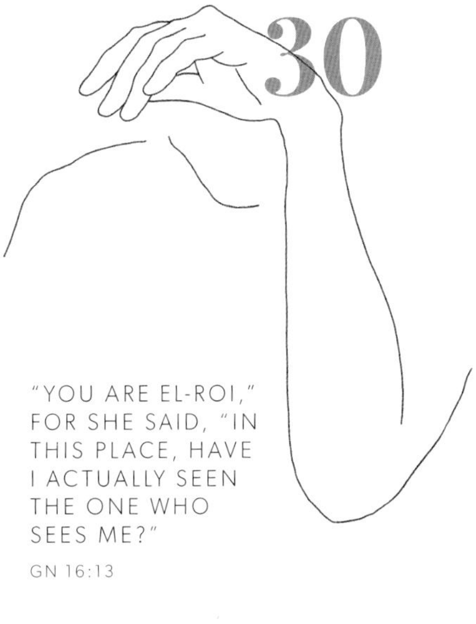

"YOU ARE EL-ROI,"
FOR SHE SAID, "IN
THIS PLACE, HAVE
I ACTUALLY SEEN
THE ONE WHO
SEES ME?"

GN 16:13

"WHO KNOWS,
PERHAPS YOU HAVE
COME TO YOUR
ROYAL POSITION
FOR SUCH A TIME
AS THIS."

EST 4:14

224

RECIPES FROM THE SHES

Each weekend features a recipe from a She in our community!

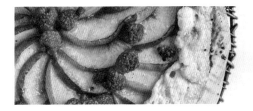

KEY VERSE

For whatever was written in the past was written for our instruction, so that we may have hope through endurance and through the encouragement from the Scriptures.

ROMANS 15:4

Women in the Word

Our mission at She Reads Truth is "Women in the Word of God every day." For eight weeks, we'll focus our Bible reading on women and men in the Old Testament—not heroes or examples to follow, but imperfect people included by God in His grand story of redemption.

WHY WOMEN AND MEN IN THE WORD?

All of the women and men in the Bible are included for a reason. No one is there by mistake. They are meant to be remembered, and we are meant to read their stories. Romans 15:4 says, "For whatever was written in the past was written for our instruction, so that we may have hope through endurance and through the encouragement from the Scriptures." The Bible, including the stories of women and men that it contains, is a gift.

WHICH WOMEN AND MEN IN THE WORD?

The women and men in this study are not the "greatest hits" of the Old Testament, and they're not a collection of unknowns either. We intentionally chose a variety of people from across the Old Testament, because every story teaches us something about God.

The women and men in this study are presented largely in chronological order. Each story stands on its own, and these readings can be revisited in any order. In many cases, we have chosen only a small portion of a person's biblical narrative. This serves to focus our time in God's Word and is not intended to minimize what we haven't included. In fact, we hope this study encourages you to take a deeper look into the lives of the people we've selected and also to read about the people we have not. Every word of Scripture is true, and every last bit important.

OUR HOPE FOR WOMEN AND MEN IN THE WORD

As "women in the Word," we want to grow and be changed by what we read. After each day's reading, you'll find questions for reflection and discussion, as well as space to respond to what God is teaching you through His Word.

The goal of this reading plan is to meet with God daily in the pages of Scripture. Our hope is that we would come to know God more deeply and worship Him wholeheartedly through reading the stories of women and men in the Bible.

How to Read the Stories of People in the Bible

The Bible is God's story, but it's also the story of women and men who played unique roles in redemption history. Some parts seem rather large, while others seem small, but every one is important.

Here are some principles to keep in mind as you read about the lives of people in the Bible.

1   **Biblical narrative is often descriptive rather than prescriptive.** Examples are not always positive or meant to be followed.

2   God spoke into culture as it existed. **Our social norms are different than those we encounter in the Bible.** It is important to remember that just because a practice is found in Scripture doesn't mean it was part of God's design for His creation.

3   **God's revelation is gradual.** Since we have the complete Old and New Testaments, we have knowledge about certain aspects of God's plan that the women and men we read about in the Old Testament did not.

4 **The Bible was written by people living in the middle of redemption history.** What they wrote was often selected to explain the circumstances God's people were experiencing in their own day.

5 **Women and men in the Bible are complex** and rarely fall into neat categories of "good" and "bad." Jesus is the only one who is truly good.

6 In the Bible, **God worked through broken, sinful people.** (He still does!)

PUNCH OUT
THE BOOKMARK
FROM THE BACK
OF YOUR BOOK
TO USE AS A
REMINDER!

Adam and Eve

God's First Image-Bearers

GENESIS 1:27

So God created man
in his own image;
he created him in the image of God;
he created them male and female.

GENESIS 2:4–9, 15–25
MAN AND WOMAN IN THE GARDEN

4 These are the records of the heavens and the earth, concerning their creation. At the time that the LORD God made the earth and the heavens, 5 no shrub of the field had yet grown on the land, and no plant of the field had yet sprouted, for the LORD God had not made it rain on the land, and there was no man to work the ground. 6 But mist would come up from the earth and water all the ground. 7 Then the LORD God formed the man out of the dust from the ground and breathed the breath of life into his nostrils, and the man became a living being.

8 The LORD God planted a garden in Eden, in the east, and there he placed the man he had formed. 9 The LORD God caused to grow out of the ground every tree pleasing in appearance and good for food, including the tree of life in the middle of the garden, as well as the tree of the knowledge of good and evil.

…

15 The LORD God took the man and placed him in the garden of Eden to work it and watch over it. 16 And the LORD God commanded the man, "You are free to eat from any tree of the garden, 17 but you must not eat from the tree of the knowledge of good and evil, for on the day you eat from it, you will certainly die." 18 Then the LORD God said, "It is not good for the man to be alone. I will make a helper corresponding to him." 19 The LORD God formed out of the ground every wild animal and every bird of the sky, and brought each to the man to see what he would call it. And whatever the man called a living creature, that was its name. 20 The man gave names to all the livestock, to the birds of the sky, and to every wild animal; but for the man no helper was found corresponding to him. 21 So the LORD God caused a deep sleep to come over the man, and he slept. God took one of his ribs and closed the flesh at that place. 22 Then the LORD God made the rib he had taken from the man into a woman and brought her to the man. 23 And the man said:

This one, at last, is bone of my bone
and flesh of my flesh;
this one will be called "woman,"
for she was taken from man.

24 This is why a man leaves his father and mother and bonds with his wife, and they become one flesh. 25 Both the man and his wife were naked, yet felt no shame.

GENESIS 3
THE TEMPTATION AND THE FALL

1 Now the serpent was the most cunning of all the wild animals that the LORD God had made. He said to the woman, "Did God really say, 'You can't eat from any tree in the garden'?"

² The woman said to the serpent, "We may eat the fruit from the trees in the garden. ³ But about the fruit of the tree in the middle of the garden, God said, 'You must not eat it or touch it, or you will die.'"

⁴ "No! You will not die," the serpent said to the woman. ⁵ "In fact, God knows that when you eat it your eyes will be opened and you will be like God, knowing good and evil." ⁶ The woman saw that the tree was good for food and delightful to look at, and that it was desirable for obtaining wisdom. So she took some of its fruit and ate it; she also gave some to her husband, who was with her, and he ate it. ⁷ Then the eyes of both of them were opened, and they knew they were naked; so they sewed fig leaves together and made coverings for themselves.

SIN'S CONSEQUENCES

⁸ Then the man and his wife heard the sound of the LORD God walking in the garden at the time of the evening breeze, and they hid from the LORD God among the trees of the garden. ⁹ So the LORD God called out to the man and said to him, "Where are you?"

¹⁰ And he said, "I heard you in the garden, and I was afraid because I was naked, so I hid."

¹¹ Then he asked, "Who told you that you were naked? Did you eat from the tree that I commanded you not to eat from?"

¹² The man replied, "The woman you gave to be with me—she gave me some fruit from the tree, and I ate."

¹³ So the LORD God asked the woman, "What is this you have done?"

And the woman said, "The serpent deceived me, and I ate."

¹⁴ So the LORD God said to the serpent:

> Because you have done this,
> you are cursed more than any livestock
> and more than any wild animal.
> You will move on your belly
> and eat dust all the days of your life.
> ¹⁵ I will put hostility between you and the woman,
> and between your offspring and her offspring.

> He will strike your head,
> and you will strike his heel.

¹⁶ He said to the woman:

> I will intensify your labor pains;
> you will bear children with painful effort.
> Your desire will be for your husband,
> yet he will rule over you.

¹⁷ And he said to the man, "Because you listened to your wife and ate from the tree about which I commanded you, 'Do not eat from it':

> The ground is cursed because of you.
> You will eat from it by means of painful labor
> all the days of your life.
> ¹⁸ It will produce thorns and thistles for you,
> and you will eat the plants of the field.
> ¹⁹ You will eat bread by the sweat of your brow
> until you return to the ground,
> since you were taken from it.
> For you are dust,
> and you will return to dust."

²⁰ The man named his wife Eve because she was the mother of all the living. ²¹ The LORD God made clothing from skins for the man and his wife, and he clothed them.

²² The LORD God said, "Since the man has become like one of us, knowing good and evil, he must not reach out, take from the tree of life, eat, and live forever." ²³ So the LORD God sent him away from the garden of Eden to work the ground from which he was taken. ²⁴ He drove the man out and stationed the cherubim and the flaming, whirling sword east of the garden of Eden to guard the way to the tree of life.

JOEL 2:26-27

²⁶ You will have plenty to eat and be satisfied.
You will praise the name of the LORD your God,
who has dealt wondrously with you.
My people will never again be put to shame.
²⁷ You will know that I am present in Israel
and that I am the LORD your God,
and there is no other.
My people will never again be put to shame.

DATE 6/3/19

1 Summarize the events of
   this story.

2 What stood out to you?
   What questions do you have?

3 What is God teaching you
   in the reading?

Noah

A Righteous Man in an Age of Wickedness

GENESIS 5:28–29

28 Lamech was 182 years old when he fathered a son. 29 And he named him Noah, saying, "This one will bring us relief from the agonizing labor of our hands, caused by the ground the LORD has cursed."

GENESIS 6:11–22

11 Now the earth was corrupt in God's sight, and the earth was filled with wickedness. 12 God saw how corrupt the earth was, for every creature had corrupted its way on the earth. 13 Then God said to Noah, "I have decided to put an end to every creature, for the earth is filled with wickedness because of them; therefore I am going to destroy them along with the earth.

14 "Make yourself an ark of gopher wood. Make rooms in the ark, and cover it with pitch inside and outside. 15 This is how you are to make it: The ark will be 450 feet long, 75 feet wide, and 45 feet high. 16 You are to make a roof, finishing the sides of the ark to within eighteen inches of the roof. You are to put a door in the side of the ark. Make it with lower, middle, and upper decks.

17 "Understand that I am bringing a flood—floodwaters on the earth to destroy every creature under heaven with the breath of life in it. Everything on earth will perish. 18 But I will establish my covenant with you, and you will enter the ark with your sons, your wife, and your sons' wives. 19 You are also to bring into the ark two of all the living creatures, male and female, to keep them alive with you. 20 Two of everything—from the birds according to their kinds, from the livestock according to their kinds, and from the animals that crawl on the ground according to their kinds—will come to you so that you can keep them alive. 21 Take with you every kind of food that is eaten; gather it as food for you and for them." 22 And Noah did this. He did everything that God had commanded him.

ENTERING THE ARK

[1] Then the LORD said to Noah, "Enter the ark, you and all your household, for I have seen that you alone are righteous before me in this generation. [2] You are to take with you seven pairs, a male and its female, of all the clean animals, and two of the animals that are not clean, a male and its female, [3] and seven pairs, male and female, of the birds of the sky—in order to keep offspring alive throughout the earth. [4] Seven days from now I will make it rain on the earth forty days and forty nights, and every living thing I have made I will wipe off the face of the earth." [5] And Noah did everything that the LORD commanded him.

[6] Noah was six hundred years old when the flood came and water covered the earth. [7] So Noah, his sons, his wife, and his sons' wives entered the ark because of the floodwaters. [8] From the clean animals, unclean animals, birds, and every creature that crawls on the ground, [9] two of each, male and female, came to Noah and entered the ark, just as God had commanded him. [10] Seven days later the floodwaters came on the earth.

THE FLOOD

[11] In the six hundredth year of Noah's life, in the second month, on the seventeenth day of the month, on that day all the sources of the vast watery depths burst open, the floodgates of the sky were opened, [12] and the rain fell on the earth forty days and forty nights.

[13] In the six hundred and first year, in the first month, on the first day of the month, the water that had covered the earth was dried up. Then Noah removed the ark's cover and saw that the surface of the ground was drying. [14] By the twenty-seventh day of the second month, the earth was dry.

THE LORD'S PROMISE

[15] Then God spoke to Noah, [16] "Come out of the ark, you, your wife, your sons, and your sons' wives with you. [17] Bring out all the living creatures that are with you—birds, livestock, those that crawl on the earth—and they will spread over the earth and be fruitful and multiply on the earth." [18] So Noah, along with his sons, his wife, and his sons' wives, came out. [19] All the animals, all the creatures that crawl, and all the flying creatures—everything that moves on the earth—came out of the ark by their families.

[20] Then Noah built an altar to the LORD. He took some of every kind of clean animal and every kind of clean bird and offered burnt offerings on the altar. [21] When the LORD smelled the pleasing aroma, he said to himself, "I will never again curse the ground because of human beings, even though the inclination of

the human heart is evil from youth onward. And I will never again strike down every living thing as I have done.

> 22 As long as the earth endures,
> seedtime and harvest, cold and heat,
> summer and winter, and day and night
> will not cease."

GENESIS 9:1–17
GOD'S COVENANT WITH NOAH

1 God blessed Noah and his sons and said to them, "Be fruitful and multiply and fill the earth. 2 The fear and terror of you will be in every living creature on the earth, every bird of the sky, every creature that crawls on the ground, and all the fish of the sea. They are placed under your authority. 3 Every creature that lives and moves will be food for you; as I gave the green plants, I have given you everything. 4 However, you must not eat meat with its lifeblood in it. 5 And I will require a penalty for your lifeblood; I will require it from any animal and from any human; if someone murders a fellow human, I will require that person's life.

> 6 Whoever sheds human blood,
> by humans his blood will be shed,
> for God made humans in his image.

7 But you, be fruitful and multiply; spread out over the earth and multiply on it."

8 Then God said to Noah and his sons with him, 9 "Understand that I am establishing my covenant with you and your descendants after you, 10 and with every living creature that is with you—birds, livestock, and all wildlife of the earth that are with you—all the animals of the earth that came out of the ark. 11 I establish my covenant with you that never again will every creature be wiped out by floodwaters; there will never again be a flood to destroy the earth."

12 And God said, "This is the sign of the covenant I am making between me and you and every living creature with you, a covenant for all future generations: 13 I have placed my bow in the clouds, and it will be a sign of the covenant between me and the earth. 14 Whenever I form clouds over the earth and the bow appears in the clouds, 15 I will remember my covenant between me and you and all the living creatures: water will never again become a flood to destroy every creature. 16 The bow will be in the clouds, and I will look at it and remember the permanent covenant between God and all the living creatures on earth." 17 God said to Noah, "This is the sign of the covenant that I have established between me and every creature on earth."

PSALM 9:10

Those who know your name trust in you
because you have not abandoned
those who seek you, LORD.

ROMANS 8:28–30

28 We know that all things work together for the good of those who love God, who are called according to his purpose. 29 For those he foreknew he also predestined to be conformed to the image of his Son, so that he would be the firstborn among many brothers and sisters. 30 And those he predestined, he also called; and those he called, he also justified; and those he justified, he also glorified.

1   Summarize the events of
    this story.

2   What stood out to you?
    What questions do you have?

3   What is God teaching you
    in the reading?

Abraham

The Father of Faith

GENESIS 11:27–31

²⁷ These are the family records of Terah. Terah fathered Abram, Nahor, and Haran, and Haran fathered Lot. ²⁸ Haran died in his native land, in Ur of the Chaldeans, during his father Terah's lifetime. ²⁹ Abram and Nahor took wives: Abram's wife was named Sarai, and Nahor's wife was named Milcah. She was the daughter of Haran, the father of both Milcah and Iscah. ³⁰ Sarai was unable to conceive; she did not have a child.

³¹ Terah took his son Abram, his grandson Lot (Haran's son), and his daughter-in-law Sarai, his son Abram's wife, and they set out together from Ur of the Chaldeans to go to the land of Canaan. But when they came to Haran, they settled there.

GENESIS 12:1–7
THE CALL OF ABRAM

¹ The Lord said to Abram:

Go out from your land,
your relatives,
and your father's house
to the land that I will show you.
² I will make you into a great nation,
I will bless you,
I will make your name great,
and you will be a blessing.
³ I will bless those who bless you,

I will curse anyone who treats you with contempt,
and all the peoples on earth
will be blessed through you.

⁴ So Abram went, as the Lord had told him, and Lot went with him. Abram was seventy-five years old when he left Haran. ⁵ He took his wife Sarai, his nephew Lot, all the possessions they had accumulated, and the people they had acquired in Haran, and they set out for the land of Canaan. When they came to the land of Canaan, ⁶ Abram passed through the land to the site of Shechem, at the oak of Moreh. (At that time the Canaanites were in the land.) ⁷ The Lord appeared to Abram and said, "To your offspring I will give this land." So he built an altar there to the Lord who had appeared to him.

GENESIS 15:1–21
THE ABRAHAMIC COVENANT

¹ After these events, the word of the Lord came to Abram in a vision:

Do not be afraid, Abram.
I am your shield;

your reward will be very great.

[2] But Abram said, "Lord GOD, what can you give me, since I am childless and the heir of my house is Eliezer of Damascus?" [3] Abram continued, "Look, you have given me no offspring, so a slave born in my house will be my heir."

[4] Now the word of the LORD came to him: "This one will not be your heir; instead, one who comes from your own body will be your heir." [5] He took him outside and said, "Look at the sky and count the stars, if you are able to count them." Then he said to him, "Your offspring will be that numerous."

[6] Abram believed the LORD, and he credited it to him as righteousness.

[7] He also said to him, "I am the LORD who brought you from Ur of the Chaldeans to give you this land to possess."

[8] But he said, "Lord GOD, how can I know that I will possess it?"

[9] He said to him, "Bring me a three-year-old cow, a three-year-old female goat, a three-year-old ram, a turtledove, and a young pigeon."

[10] So he brought all these to him, cut them in half, and laid the pieces opposite each other, but he did not cut the birds in half. [11] Birds of prey came down on the carcasses, but Abram drove them away. [12] As the sun was setting, a deep sleep came over Abram, and suddenly great terror and darkness descended on him.

[13] Then the LORD said to Abram, "Know this for certain: Your offspring will be resident aliens for four hundred years in a land that does not belong to them and will be enslaved and oppressed. [14] However, I will judge the nation they serve, and afterward they will go out with many possessions. [15] But you will go to your fathers in peace and be buried at a good old age. [16] In the fourth generation they will return here, for the iniquity of the Amorites has not yet reached its full measure."

[17] When the sun had set and it was dark, a smoking fire pot and a flaming torch appeared and passed between the divided animals. [18] On that day the LORD made a covenant with Abram, saying, "I give this land to your offspring, from the Brook of Egypt to the great river, the Euphrates River: [19] the land of the Kenites, Kenizzites, Kadmonites, [20] Hethites, Perizzites, Rephaim, [21] Amorites, Canaanites, Girgashites, and Jebusites."

GENESIS 17:1–14, 23–37
COVENANT CIRCUMCISION

[1] When Abram was ninety-nine years old, the LORD appeared to him, saying, "I am God Almighty. Live in my presence and be blameless. [2] I will set up my covenant between me and you, and I will multiply you greatly."

"Do not be afraid, Abram. I am your shield."

———

³ Then Abram fell facedown and God spoke with him: ⁴ "As for me, here is my covenant with you: You will become the father of many nations. ⁵ Your name will no longer be Abram; your name will be Abraham, for I will make you the father of many nations. ⁶ I will make you extremely fruitful and will make nations and kings come from you. ⁷ I will confirm my covenant that is between me and you and your future offspring throughout their generations. It is a permanent covenant to be your God and the God of your offspring after you. ⁸ And to you and your future offspring I will give the land where you are residing—all the land of Canaan—as a permanent possession, and I will be their God."

⁹ God also said to Abraham, "As for you, you and your offspring after you throughout their generations are to keep my covenant. ¹⁰ This is my covenant between me and you and your offspring after you, which you are to keep: Every one of your males must be circumcised. ¹¹ You must circumcise the flesh of your foreskin to serve as a sign of the covenant between me and you. ¹² Throughout your generations, every male among you is to be circumcised at eight days old—every male born in your household or purchased from any foreigner and not your offspring. ¹³ Whether born in your household or purchased, he must be circumcised. My covenant will be marked in your flesh as a permanent covenant. ¹⁴ If any male is not circumcised in the flesh of his foreskin, that man will be cut off from his people; he has broken my covenant."

...

²³ So Abraham took his son Ishmael and those born in his household or purchased—every male among the members of Abraham's household—and he circumcised the flesh of their foreskin on that very day, just as God had said to him. ²⁴ Abraham was ninety-nine years old when the flesh of his foreskin was circumcised, ²⁵ and his son Ishmael was thirteen years old when the flesh of his foreskin was circumcised. ²⁶ On that same day Abraham and his son Ishmael were circumcised. ²⁷ And all the men of his household—whether born in his household or purchased from a foreigner—were circumcised with him.

GALATIANS 3:8

Now the Scripture saw in advance that God would justify the Gentiles by faith and proclaimed the gospel ahead of time to Abraham, saying, All the nations will be blessed through you.

1 Summarize the events of
this story.

2 What stood out to you?
What questions do you have?

3 What is God teaching you
in the reading?

Hagar

The Woman Seen by God

HAGAR AND ISHMAEL

[1] Abram's wife Sarai had not borne any children for him, but she owned an Egyptian slave named Hagar. [2] Sarai said to Abram, "Since the LORD has prevented me from bearing children, go to my slave; perhaps through her I can build a family." And Abram agreed to what Sarai said. [3] So Abram's wife Sarai took Hagar, her Egyptian slave, and gave her to her husband Abram as a wife for him. This happened after Abram had lived in the land of Canaan ten years. [4] He slept with Hagar, and she became pregnant. When she saw that she was pregnant, her mistress became contemptible to her. [5] Then Sarai said to Abram, "You are responsible for my suffering! I put my slave in your arms, and when she saw that she was pregnant, I became contemptible to her. May the LORD judge between me and you."

[6] Abram replied to Sarai, "Here, your slave is in your hands; do whatever you want with her." Then Sarai mistreated her so much that she ran away from her.

[7] The angel of the LORD found her by a spring in the wilderness, the spring on the way to Shur. [8] He said, "Hagar, slave of Sarai, where have you come from and where are you going?"

She replied, "I'm running away from my mistress Sarai."

[9] The angel of the LORD said to her, "Go back to your mistress and submit to her authority." [10] The angel of the LORD said to her, "I will greatly multiply your offspring, and they will be too many to count."

[11] The angel of the LORD said to her, "You have conceived and will have a son. You will name him Ishmael, for the LORD has heard your cry of affliction. [12] This man will be like a wild donkey. His hand will be against everyone, and everyone's hand will be against him; he will settle near all his relatives."

[13] So she named the LORD who spoke to her: "You are El-roi," for she said, "In this place, have I actually seen the one who sees me?" [14] That is why the well is called Beer-lahai-roi. It is between Kadesh and Bered.

[15] So Hagar gave birth to Abram's son, and Abram named his son (whom Hagar bore) Ishmael. [16] Abram was eighty-six years old when Hagar bore Ishmael to him.

HAGAR AND ISHMAEL SENT AWAY

[8] The child grew and was weaned, and Abraham held a great feast on the day Isaac was weaned. [9] But Sarah saw the son mocking—the one Hagar the Egyptian had

borne to Abraham. ¹⁰ So she said to Abraham, "Drive out this slave with her son, for the son of this slave will not be a coheir with my son Isaac!"

¹¹ This was very distressing to Abraham because of his son. ¹² But God said to Abraham, "Do not be distressed about the boy and about your slave. Whatever Sarah says to you, listen to her, because your offspring will be traced through Isaac, ¹³ and I will also make a nation of the slave's son because he is your offspring."

¹⁴ Early in the morning Abraham got up, took bread and a waterskin, put them on Hagar's shoulders, and sent her and the boy away. She left and wandered in the Wilderness of Beer-sheba. ¹⁵ When the water in the skin was gone, she left the boy under one of the bushes ¹⁶ and went and sat at a distance, about a bowshot away, for she said, "I can't bear to watch the boy die!" While she sat at a distance, she wept loudly.

———

GENESIS 16:13

So she named the LORD who spoke to her: "You are El-roi," for she said, "In this place, have I actually seen the one who sees me?"

———

¹⁷ God heard the boy crying, and the angel of God called to Hagar from heaven and said to her, "What's wrong, Hagar? Don't be afraid, for God has heard the boy crying from the place where he is. ¹⁸ Get up, help the boy up, and grasp his hand, for I will make him a great nation." ¹⁹ Then God opened her eyes, and she saw a well. So she went and filled the waterskin and gave the boy a drink. ²⁰ God was with the boy, and he grew; he settled in the wilderness and became an archer. ²¹ He settled in the Wilderness of Paran, and his mother got a wife for him from the land of Egypt.

PSALM 56:8

You yourself have recorded my wanderings.
Put my tears in your bottle.
Are they not in your book?

1   Summarize the events of
    this story.

2   What stood out to you?
    What questions do you have?

3   What is God teaching you
    in the reading?

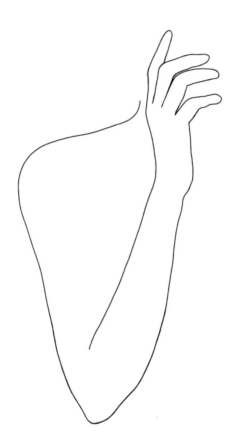

Sarah

The Mother of the Promise

[15] God said to Abraham, "As for your wife Sarai, do not call her Sarai, for Sarah will be her name. [16] I will bless her; indeed, I will give you a son by her. I will bless her, and she will produce nations; kings of peoples will come from her."

[17] Abraham fell facedown. Then he laughed and said to himself, "Can a child be born to a hundred-year-old man? Can Sarah, a ninety-year-old woman, give birth?" [18] So Abraham said to God, "If only Ishmael were acceptable to you!"

[19] But God said, "No. Your wife Sarah will bear you a son, and you will name him Isaac. I will confirm my covenant with him as a permanent covenant for his future offspring." [20] As for Ishmael, I have heard you. I will certainly bless him; I will make him fruitful and will multiply him greatly. He will father twelve tribal leaders, and I will make him into a great nation. [21] But I will confirm my covenant with Isaac, whom Sarah will bear to you at this time next year." [22] When he finished talking with him, God withdrew from Abraham.

GENESIS 18:1–15
ABRAHAM'S THREE VISITORS

[1] The LORD appeared to Abraham at the oaks of Mamre while he was sitting at the entrance of his tent during the heat of the day. [2] He looked up, and he saw three men standing near him. When he saw them, he ran from the entrance of the tent to meet them, bowed to the ground, [3] and said, "My lord, if I have found favor with you, please do not go on past your servant. [4] Let a little water be brought, that you may wash your feet and rest yourselves under the tree. [5] I will bring a bit of bread so that you may strengthen yourselves. This is why you have passed your servant's way. Later, you can continue on."

"Yes," they replied, "do as you have said."

[6] So Abraham hurried into the tent and said to Sarah, "Quick! Knead three measures of fine flour and make bread." [7] Abraham ran to the herd and got a tender, choice calf. He gave it to a young man, who hurried to prepare it. [8] Then Abraham took curds and milk, as well as the calf that he had prepared, and set them before the men. He served them as they ate under the tree.

SARAH LAUGHS

[9] "Where is your wife Sarah?" they asked him.

"There, in the tent," he answered.

[10] The LORD said, "I will certainly come back to you in about a year's time, and your wife Sarah will have a son!" Now Sarah was listening at the entrance of the tent behind him.

[11] Abraham and Sarah were old and getting on in years. Sarah had passed the age of childbearing. [12] So she laughed to herself: "After I am worn out and my lord is old, will I have delight?"

[13] But the LORD asked Abraham, "Why did Sarah laugh, saying, 'Can I really have a baby when I'm old?' [14] Is anything impossible for the LORD? At the appointed time I will come back to you, and in about a year she will have a son."

[15] Sarah denied it. "I did not laugh," she said, because she was afraid.

But he replied, "No, you did laugh."

GENESIS 20
SARAH RESCUED FROM ABIMELECH

[1] From there Abraham traveled to the region of the Negev and settled between Kadesh and Shur. While he was staying in Gerar, [2] Abraham said about his wife Sarah, "She is my sister." So King Abimelech of Gerar had Sarah brought to him.

[3] But God came to Abimelech in a dream by night and said to him, "You are about to die because of the woman you have taken, for she is a married woman."

[4] Now Abimelech had not approached her, so he said, "Lord, would you destroy a nation even though it is innocent? [5] Didn't he himself say to me, 'She is my sister'? And she

Sarah said, "God has made me laugh, and everyone who hears will laugh with me."

herself said, 'He is my brother.' I did this with a clear conscience and clean hands."

⁶ Then God said to him in the dream, "Yes, I know that you did this with a clear conscience. I have also kept you from sinning against me. Therefore I have not let you touch her. ⁷ Now return the man's wife, for he is a prophet, and he will pray for you and you will live. But if you do not return her, know that you will certainly die, you and all who are yours."

⁸ Early in the morning Abimelech got up, called all his servants together, and personally told them all these things, and the men were terrified.

⁹ Then Abimelech called Abraham in and said to him, "What have you done to us? How did I sin against you that you have brought such enormous guilt on me and on my kingdom? You have done things to me that should never be done." ¹⁰ Abimelech also asked Abraham, "What made you do this?"

¹¹ Abraham replied, "I thought, 'There is absolutely no fear of God in this place. They will kill me because of my wife.' ¹² Besides, she really is my sister, the daughter of my father though not the daughter of my mother, and she became my wife. ¹³ So when God had me wander from my father's house, I said to her: Show your loyalty to me wherever we go and say about me: 'He's my brother.'"

¹⁴ Then Abimelech took flocks and herds and male and female slaves, gave them to Abraham, and returned his wife Sarah to him. ¹⁵ Abimelech said, "Look, my land is before you. Settle wherever you want." ¹⁶ And he said to Sarah,

"Look, I am giving your brother one thousand pieces of silver. It is a verification of your honor to all who are with you. You are fully vindicated."

¹⁷ Then Abraham prayed to God, and God healed Abimelech, his wife, and his female slaves so that they could bear children, ¹⁸ for the LORD had completely closed all the wombs in Abimelech's household on account of Sarah, Abraham's wife.

GENESIS 21:1–7
THE BIRTH OF ISAAC

¹ The LORD came to Sarah as he had said, and the LORD did for Sarah what he had promised. ² Sarah became pregnant and bore a son to Abraham in his old age, at the appointed time God had told him. ³ Abraham named his son who was born to him—the one Sarah bore to him—Isaac. ⁴ When his son Isaac was eight days old, Abraham circumcised him, as God had commanded him. ⁵ Abraham was a hundred years old when his son Isaac was born to him.

⁶ Sarah said, "God has made me laugh, and everyone who hears will laugh with me." ⁷ She also said, "Who would have told Abraham that Sarah would nurse children? Yet I have borne a son for him in his old age."

PHILIPPIANS 1:6

I am sure of this, that he who started a good work in you will carry it on to completion until the day of Christ Jesus.

1   Summarize the events of
     this story.

2   What stood out to you?
     What questions do you have?

3   What is God teaching you
     in the reading?

Peach Frozen Yogurt Breakfast Pops

PREP TIME	COOK TIME	FREEZE TIME	SERVINGS
10 minutes	10 minutes	12–24 hours	16 popsicles

INGREDIENTS

PEACH PUREE

4 large peaches

½ inch piece fresh ginger, peeled

¼ teaspoon ground cinnamon

2 tablespoons fresh lemon juice

¼ cup brown sugar, packed

POPSICLE BASE

32 ounces plain Greek yogurt

¼–½ cup honey

½ cup honey-almond granola

MARTA RIVERA

@senseandedibility

DIRECTIONS

Use a sharp paring knife to score an X on the bottom of each peach. Grab the point of the skin between the flat side of the knife and the thumb on your dominant hand to remove the skin of the peach. Discard the peach skins.

Cut fruit in half and remove hard pits.

Dice peach halves and set aside ½ cup.

Place remaining peaches in a saucepan, then grate the ginger root into the pan. Add the cinnamon, lemon juice, and brown sugar to the pot and bring this mixture to a simmer over medium-low heat. Cook until the peaches begin to soften and fall apart—about 10 minutes.

Remove the pot from the stove and puree peach mixture until smooth using an immersion blender (or transfer to a blender). Cool to room temperature.

To make the yogurt base, stir honey into the yogurt to sweeten it. Start with ¼ cup of honey. For a sweeter taste, add up to ½ cup of honey.

Add the room temperature peach puree to the sweetened yogurt and use a rubber spatula to fold it in.

Spoon the mixture into the cavities of a silicone or plastic popsicle mold, filling each ¼ full. Add a tablespoon of the reserved peach pieces.

Top with more yogurt mix, leaving a space ⅓ from the top of the cavity.

Add 1 or 2 tablespoons of granola and press a bit to compact it. Top with a teaspoon of the mixture to bind the granola. Cover and allow the popsicles to freeze for 12 to 24 hours.

To serve, run hot water over the mold. If you have silicone molds, gently loosen them by pulling the silicone away from the frozen popsicles.

Wrap your popsicles in freezer-safe wax paper, or place them in popsicle bags. Store in the freezer for up to two months.

Grace Day

Use this day to pray, rest, and reflect on this week's reading,
giving thanks for the grace that is ours in Christ.

I am sure of this, that he who started a good work in you will carry it on to completion until the day of Christ Jesus.

Scripture is God-breathed and true. When we memorize it, we carry the gospel with us wherever we go.

This week we'll memorize Romans 8:28, a reminder that the same God who is sovereign over these stories in the Old Testament is sovereign over our stories as well.

Weekly Truth

ROMANS 8:28

We know that all things work together for the good of those who love God, who are called according to his purpose.

Find the corresponding memory card in the back of this book.

Isaac

The Son Offered Up to God

GENESIS 22:1-19

THE SACRIFICE OF ISAAC

[1] After these things God tested Abraham and said to him, "Abraham!"

"Here I am," he answered.

[2] "Take your son," he said, "your only son Isaac, whom you love, go to the land of Moriah, and offer him there as a burnt offering on one of the mountains I will tell you about."

[3] So Abraham got up early in the morning, saddled his donkey, and took with him two of his young men and his son Isaac. He split wood for a burnt offering and set out to go to the place God had told him about. [4] On the third day Abraham looked up and saw the place in the distance. [5] Then Abraham said to his young men, "Stay here with the donkey. The boy and I will go over there to worship; then we'll come back to you." [6] Abraham took the wood for the burnt offering and laid it on his son Isaac. In his hand he took the fire and the knife, and the two of them walked on together.

[7] Then Isaac spoke to his father Abraham and said, "My father."

And he replied, "Here I am, my son."

Isaac said, "The fire and the wood are here, but where is the lamb for the burnt offering?"

[8] Abraham answered, "God himself will provide the lamb for the burnt offering, my son." Then the two of them walked on together.

[9] When they arrived at the place that God had told him about, Abraham built the altar there and arranged the wood. He bound his son Isaac and placed him on the altar on top of the wood. [10] Then Abraham reached out and took the knife to slaughter his son.

NOTES

11 But the angel of the LORD called to him from heaven and said, "Abraham,
Abraham!"

He replied, "Here I am."

12 Then he said, "Do not lay a hand on the boy or do anything to him. For now
I know that you fear God, since you have not withheld your only son from me."
13 Abraham looked up and saw a ram caught in the thicket by its horns. So
Abraham went and took the ram and offered it as a burnt offering in place of his
son. 14 And Abraham named that place The LORD Will Provide, so today it is said:
"It will be provided on the LORD's mountain."

15 Then the angel of the LORD called to Abraham a second time from heaven
16 and said, "By myself I have sworn," this is the LORD's declaration: "Because you
have done this thing and have not withheld your only son, 17 I will indeed bless
you and make your offspring as numerous as the stars of the sky and the sand on
the seashore. Your offspring will possess the city gates of their enemies. 18 And all
the nations of the earth will be blessed by your offspring because you have obeyed
my command."

19 Abraham went back to his young men, and they got up and went together to
Beer-sheba. And Abraham settled in Beer-sheba.

GENESIS 25:11

After Abraham's death, God blessed his son Isaac, who lived near Beer-lahai-roi.

GENESIS 26:1–5, 12–25

THE PROMISE REAFFIRMED TO ISAAC

1 There was another famine in the land in addition to the one that had occurred
in Abraham's time. And Isaac went to Abimelech, king of the Philistines, at Gerar.
2 The LORD appeared to him and said, "Do not go down to Egypt. Live in the land
that I tell you about; 3 stay in this land as an alien, and I will be with you and bless
you. For I will give all these lands to you and your offspring, and I will confirm the
oath that I swore to your father Abraham. 4 I will make your offspring as numerous
as the stars of the sky, I will give your offspring all these lands, and all the nations of
the earth will be blessed by your offspring, 5 because Abraham listened to me and
kept my mandate, my commands, my statutes, and my instructions."

...

CONFLICTS OVER WELLS

12 Isaac sowed seed in that land, and in that year he reaped a hundred times what
was sown. The LORD blessed him, 13 and the man became rich and kept getting
richer until he was very wealthy. 14 He had flocks of sheep, herds of cattle, and

many slaves, and the Philistines were envious of him. [15] Philistines stopped up all the wells that his father's servants had dug in the days of his father Abraham, filling them with dirt. [16] And Abimelech said to Isaac, "Leave us, for you are much too powerful for us."

[17] So Isaac left there, camped in the Gerar Valley, and lived there. [18] Isaac reopened the wells that had been dug in the days of his father Abraham and that the Philistines had stopped up after Abraham died. He gave them the same names his father had given them. [19] Then Isaac's servants dug in the valley and found a well of spring water there. [20] But the herdsmen of Gerar quarreled with Isaac's herdsmen and said, "The water is ours!" So he named the well Esek because they argued with him. [21] Then they dug another well and quarreled over that one also, so he named it Sitnah. [22] He moved from there and dug another, and they did not quarrel over it. He named it Rehoboth and said, "For now the Lord has made space for us, and we will be fruitful in the land."

———

GENESIS 22:7

Isaac said, "The fire and the wood are here, but where is the lamb for the burnt offering?"

———

THE LORD APPEARS TO ISAAC

[23] From there he went up to Beer-sheba, [24] and the Lord appeared to him that night and said, "I am the God of your father Abraham. Do not be afraid, for I am with you. I will bless you and multiply your offspring because of my servant Abraham."

[25] So he built an altar there, called on the name of the Lord, and pitched his tent there. Isaac's servants also dug a well there.

JOHN 3:16–17

[16] "For God loved the world in this way: He gave his one and only Son, so that everyone who believes in him will not perish but have eternal life. [17] For God did not send his Son into the world to condemn the world, but to save the world through him."

1 Summarize the events of
this story.

2 What stood out to you?
What questions do you have?

3 What is God teaching you
in the reading?

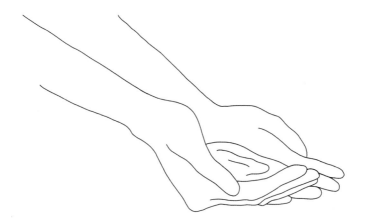

Rebekah

The Woman Who Left Everything Familiar Behind

A WIFE FOR ISAAC

[1] Abraham was now old, getting on in years, and the LORD had blessed him in everything. [2] Abraham said to his servant, the elder of his household who managed all he owned, "Place your hand under my thigh, [3] and I will have you swear by the LORD, God of heaven and God of earth, that you will not take a wife for my son from the daughters of the Canaanites among whom I live, [4] but will go to my land and my family to take a wife for my son Isaac."

[5] The servant said to him, "Suppose the woman is unwilling to follow me to this land? Should I have your son go back to the land you came from?"

[6] Abraham answered him, "Make sure that you don't take my son back there. [7] The LORD, the God of heaven, who took me from my father's house and from my native land, who spoke to me and swore to me, 'I will give this land to your offspring'—he will send his angel before you, and you can take a wife for my son from there. [8] If the woman is unwilling to follow you, then you are free from this oath to me, but don't let my son go back there." [9] So the servant placed his hand under his master Abraham's thigh and swore an oath to him concerning this matter.

[10] The servant took ten of his master's camels, and with all kinds of his master's goods in hand, he went to Aram-naharaim, to Nahor's town. [11] At evening, the time when women went out to draw water, he made the camels kneel beside a well outside the town.

[12] "LORD, God of my master Abraham," he prayed, "make this happen for me today, and show kindness to my master Abraham. [13] I am standing here at the spring where the daughters of the men of the town are coming out to draw water. [14] Let the girl to whom I say, 'Please lower your water jug so that I may drink,' and who responds, 'Drink, and I'll water your camels also'—let her be the one you have appointed for your servant Isaac. By this I will know that you have shown kindness to my master."

[15] Before he had finished speaking, there was Rebekah—daughter of Bethuel son of Milcah, the wife of Abraham's brother Nahor—coming with a jug on her shoulder. [16] Now the girl was very beautiful, a virgin—no man had been intimate with her. She went down to the spring, filled her jug, and came up. [17] Then the servant ran to meet her and said, "Please let me have a little water from your jug."

[18] She replied, "Drink, my lord." She quickly lowered her jug to her hand and gave him a drink. [19] When she had finished giving him a drink, she said, "I'll also draw water for your camels until they have had enough to drink." [20] She quickly emptied her jug into the trough and hurried to the well again to draw water. She drew water

Rebekah is here in front of you. Take her and go, and let her be a wife for your master's son, just as the LORD has spoken.

⸺

for all his camels ²¹ while the man silently watched her to see whether or not the LORD had made his journey a success.

²² As the camels finished drinking, the man took a gold ring weighing half a shekel, and for her wrists two bracelets weighing ten shekels of gold. ²³ "Whose daughter are you?" he asked. "Please tell me, is there room in your father's house for us to spend the night?"

²⁴ She answered him, "I am the daughter of Bethuel son of Milcah, whom she bore to Nahor." ²⁵ She also said to him, "We have plenty of straw and feed and a place to spend the night."

²⁶ Then the man knelt low, worshiped the LORD, ²⁷ and said, "Blessed be the LORD, the God of my master Abraham, who has not withheld his kindness and faithfulness from my master. As for me, the LORD has led me on the journey to the house of my master's relatives."

²⁸ The girl ran and told her mother's household about these things. ²⁹ Now Rebekah had a brother named Laban, and Laban ran out to the man at the spring. ³⁰ As soon as he had seen the ring and the bracelets on his sister's wrists, and when he had heard his sister Rebekah's words—"The man said this to me!"—he went to the man. He was standing there by the camels at the spring.

³¹ Laban said, "Come, you who are blessed by the LORD. Why are you standing out here? I have prepared the house and a place for the camels." ³² So the man came to the house, and the camels were unloaded. Straw and feed were given to the camels, and water was brought to wash his feet and the feet of the men with him.

³³ A meal was set before him, but he said, "I will not eat until I have said what I have to say."

So Laban said, "Please speak."

³⁴ "I am Abraham's servant," he said. ³⁵ "The LORD has greatly blessed my master, and he has become rich. He has given him flocks and herds, silver and gold, male and female slaves, and camels and donkeys. ³⁶ Sarah, my master's wife, bore a son to my master in her old age, and he has given him everything he owns. ³⁷ My master put me under this oath: 'You will not take a wife for my son from the daughters of the Canaanites in whose land I live ³⁸ but will go to my father's family and to my clan to take a wife for my son.' ³⁹ But I said to my master, 'Suppose the woman will not come back with me?' ⁴⁰ He said to me, 'The LORD before whom I have walked will send his angel with you and make your journey a success, and you will take a wife for my son from my clan and from my father's family. ⁴¹ Then you will be free from my oath if you go to my family and they do not give her to you—you will be free from my oath.'

⁴² "Today when I came to the spring, I prayed: LORD, God of my master Abraham, if only you will make my journey successful! ⁴³ I am standing here at a spring. Let the young woman who comes out to draw water, and I say to her, 'Please let me drink a little water from your jug,' ⁴⁴ and who

responds to me, 'Drink, and I'll draw water for your camels also'—let her be the woman the LORD has appointed for my master's son.

⁴⁵ "Before I had finished praying silently, there was Rebekah coming with her jug on her shoulder, and she went down to the spring and drew water. So I said to her, 'Please let me have a drink.' ⁴⁶ She quickly lowered her jug from her shoulder and said, 'Drink, and I'll water your camels also.' So I drank, and she also watered the camels. ⁴⁷ Then I asked her, 'Whose daughter are you?' She responded, 'The daughter of Bethuel son of Nahor, whom Milcah bore to him.' So I put the ring on her nose and the bracelets on her wrists. ⁴⁸ Then I knelt low, worshiped the LORD, and blessed the LORD, the God of my master Abraham, who guided me on the right way to take the granddaughter of my master's brother for his son. ⁴⁹ Now, if you are going to show kindness and faithfulness to my master, tell me; if not, tell me, and I will go elsewhere."

⁵⁰ Laban and Bethuel answered, "This is from the LORD; we have no choice in the matter. ⁵¹ Rebekah is here in front of you. Take her and go, and let her be a wife for your master's son, just as the LORD has spoken."

⁵² When Abraham's servant heard their words, he bowed to the ground before the LORD. ⁵³ Then he brought out objects of silver and gold, and garments, and gave them to Rebekah. He also gave precious gifts to her brother and her mother. ⁵⁴ Then he and the men with him ate and drank and spent the night.

When they got up in the morning, he said, "Send me to my master."

⁵⁵ But her brother and mother said, "Let the girl stay with us for about ten days. Then she can go."

⁵⁶ But he responded to them, "Do not delay me, since the LORD has made my journey a success. Send me away so that I may go to my master."

⁵⁷ So they said, "Let's call the girl and ask her opinion."

⁵⁸ They called Rebekah and said to her, "Will you go with this man?"

She replied, "I will go." ⁵⁹ So they sent away their sister Rebekah with the one who had nursed and raised her, and Abraham's servant and his men.

⁶⁰ They blessed Rebekah, saying to her:

> Our sister, may you become
> thousands upon ten thousands.
> May your offspring possess
> the city gates of their enemies.

[61] Then Rebekah and her female servants got up, mounted the camels, and followed the man. So the servant took Rebekah and left.

[62] Now Isaac was returning from Beer-lahai-roi, for he was living in the Negev region. [63] In the early evening Isaac went out to walk in the field, and looking up he saw camels coming. [64] Rebekah looked up, and when she saw Isaac, she got down from her camel [65] and asked the servant, "Who is that man in the field coming to meet us?"

The servant answered, "It is my master." So she took her veil and covered herself. [66] Then the servant told Isaac everything he had done.

[67] And Isaac brought her into the tent of his mother Sarah and took Rebekah to be his wife. Isaac loved her, and he was comforted after his mother's death.

GENESIS 25:19–26

THE BIRTH OF JACOB AND ESAU

[19] These are the family records of Isaac son of Abraham. Abraham fathered Isaac. [20] Isaac was forty years old when he took as his wife Rebekah daughter of Bethuel the Aramean from Paddan-aram and sister of Laban the Aramean. [21] Isaac prayed to the LORD on behalf of his wife because she was childless. The LORD was receptive to his prayer, and his wife Rebekah conceived. [22] But the children inside her struggled with each other, and she said, "Why is this happening to me?" So she went to inquire of the LORD. [23] And the LORD said to her:

> Two nations are in your womb;
> two peoples will come from you and be separated.
> One people will be stronger than the other,
> and the older will serve the younger.

[24] When her time came to give birth, there were indeed twins in her womb. [25] The first one came out red-looking, covered with hair like a fur coat, and they named him Esau. [26] After this, his brother came out grasping Esau's heel with his hand. So he was named Jacob. Isaac was sixty years old when they were born.

PSALM 37:23–24

[23] A person's steps are established by the LORD,
and he takes pleasure in his way.
[24] Though he falls, he will not be overwhelmed,
because the LORD supports him with his hand.

1   Summarize the events of
    this story.

2   What stood out to you?
    What questions do you have?

3   What is God teaching you
    in the reading?

Esau

The Son Who Traded His Birthright for Stew

GENESIS 25:27–34

ESAU SELLS HIS BIRTHRIGHT

²⁷ When the boys grew up, Esau became an expert hunter, an outdoorsman, but Jacob was a quiet man who stayed at home. ²⁸ Isaac loved Esau because he had a taste for wild game, but Rebekah loved Jacob.

²⁹ Once when Jacob was cooking a stew, Esau came in from the field exhausted. ³⁰ He said to Jacob, "Let me eat some of that red stuff, because I'm exhausted." That is why he was also named Edom.

³¹ Jacob replied, "First sell me your birthright."

³² "Look," said Esau, "I'm about to die, so what good is a birthright to me?"

³³ Jacob said, "Swear to me first." So he swore to Jacob and sold his birthright to him. ³⁴ Then Jacob gave bread and lentil stew to Esau; he ate, drank, got up, and went away. So Esau despised his birthright.

GENESIS 26:34–35

ESAU'S WIVES

³⁴ When Esau was forty years old, he took as his wives Judith daughter of Beeri the Hethite, and Basemath daughter of Elon the Hethite. ³⁵ They made life bitter for Isaac and Rebekah.

GENESIS 27

THE STOLEN BLESSING

¹ When Isaac was old and his eyes were so weak that he could not see, he called his older son Esau and said to him, "My son."

And he answered, "Here I am."

² He said, "Look, I am old and do not know the day of my death. ³ So now take your hunting gear, your quiver and bow, and go out in the field to hunt some game for me. ⁴ Then make me a delicious meal that I love and bring it to me to eat, so that I can bless you before I die."

⁵ Now Rebekah was listening to what Isaac said to his son Esau. So while Esau went to the field to hunt some game to bring in, ⁶ Rebekah said to her son Jacob, "Listen! I heard your father talking with your brother Esau. He said, ⁷ 'Bring me game and make a delicious meal for me to eat so that I can bless you in the Lᴏʀᴅ's presence before I die.' ⁸ Now, my son, listen to me and do what I tell you. ⁹ Go to the flock and bring me two choice young goats, and I will make them into a delicious meal for your father—the kind he loves. ¹⁰ Then take it to your father to eat so that he may bless you before he dies."

¹¹ Jacob answered Rebekah his mother, "Look, my brother Esau is a hairy man, but I am a man with smooth skin. ¹² Suppose my father touches me. Then I will be revealed to

him as a deceiver and bring a curse rather than a blessing on myself."

¹³ His mother said to him, "Your curse be on me, my son. Just obey me and go get them for me."

¹⁴ So he went and got the goats and brought them to his mother, and his mother made the delicious food his father loved. ¹⁵ Then Rebekah took the best clothes of her older son Esau, which were in the house, and had her younger son Jacob wear them. ¹⁶ She put the skins of the young goats on his hands and the smooth part of his neck. ¹⁷ Then she handed the delicious food and the bread she had made to her son Jacob.

¹⁸ When he came to his father, he said, "My father."

And he answered, "Here I am. Who are you, my son?"

¹⁹ Jacob replied to his father, "I am Esau, your firstborn. I have done as you told me. Please sit up and eat some of my game so that you may bless me."

²⁰ But Isaac said to his son, "How did you ever find it so quickly, my son?"

He replied, "Because the LORD your God made it happen for me."

²¹ Then Isaac said to Jacob, "Please come closer so I can touch you, my son. Are you really my son Esau or not?"

²² So Jacob came closer to his father Isaac. When he touched him, he said, "The voice is the voice of Jacob, but the hands are the hands of Esau." ²³ He did not recognize him, because his hands were hairy like those of his brother Esau; so he blessed him. ²⁴ Again he asked, "Are you really my son Esau?"

And he replied, "I am."

²⁵ Then he said, "Bring it closer to me, and let me eat some of my son's game so that I can bless you." Jacob brought it closer to him, and he ate; he brought him wine, and he drank.

²⁶ Then his father Isaac said to him, "Please come closer and kiss me, my son." ²⁷ So he came closer and kissed him. When Isaac smelled his clothes, he blessed him and said:

Ah, the smell of my son
is like the smell of a field
that the LORD has blessed.
²⁸ May God give to you—
from the dew of the sky
and from the richness of the land—
an abundance of grain and new wine.
²⁹ May peoples serve you
and nations bow in worship to you.
Be master over your relatives;
may your mother's sons bow in worship to you.
Those who curse you will be cursed,
and those who bless you will be blessed.

³⁰ As soon as Isaac had finished blessing Jacob and Jacob had left the presence of his father Isaac, his brother Esau arrived from his hunting. ³¹ He had also made some delicious food and brought it to his father. He said to his father, "Let my father get up and eat some of his son's game, so that you may bless me."

³² But his father Isaac said to him, "Who are you?"

He answered, "I am Esau your firstborn son."

³³ Isaac began to tremble uncontrollably. "Who was it then," he said, "who hunted game and brought it to me? I ate it all before you came in, and I blessed him. Indeed, he will be blessed!"

³⁴ When Esau heard his father's words, he cried out with a loud and bitter cry and said to his father, "Bless me too, my father!"

³⁵ But he replied, "Your brother came deceitfully and took your blessing."

³⁶ So he said, "Isn't he rightly named Jacob? For he has cheated me twice now. He took my birthright, and look, now he has taken my blessing." Then he asked, "Haven't you saved a blessing for me?"

³⁷ But Isaac answered Esau, "Look, I have made him a master over you, have given him all of his relatives as his servants, and have sustained him with grain and new wine. What then can I do for you, my son?"

³⁸ Esau said to his father, "Do you have only one blessing, my father? Bless me too, my father!" And Esau wept loudly.

³⁹ His father Isaac answered him,

> Look, your dwelling place will be
> away from the richness of the land,
> away from the dew of the sky above.
> ⁴⁰ You will live by your sword,
> and you will serve your brother.
> But when you rebel,
> you will break his yoke from your neck.

ESAU'S ANGER

⁴¹ Esau held a grudge against Jacob because of the blessing his father had given him. And Esau determined in his heart: "The days of mourning for my father are approaching; then I will kill my brother Jacob."

⁴² When the words of her older son Esau were reported to Rebekah, she summoned her younger son Jacob and said to him, "Listen, your brother Esau is consoling himself by planning to kill you. ⁴³ So now, my son, listen to me. Flee at once to my brother Laban in Haran, ⁴⁴ and stay with him for a few days until your brother's anger subsides— ⁴⁵ until your brother's rage turns away from you and he forgets what you have done to him. Then I will send for you and bring you back from there. Why should I lose you both in one day?"

⁴⁶ So Rebekah said to Isaac, "I'm sick of my life because of these Hethite girls. If Jacob marries someone from around here, like these Hethite girls, what good is my life?"

GENESIS 28:1–5
JACOB'S DEPARTURE

¹ So Isaac summoned Jacob, blessed him, and commanded him, "Do not marry a Canaanite girl. ² Go at once to Paddan-aram, to the house of Bethuel, your mother's father. Marry one of the daughters of Laban, your mother's brother. ³ May God Almighty bless you and make you fruitful and multiply you so that you become an assembly of peoples. ⁴ May God give you and your offspring the blessing of Abraham so that you may possess the land where you live as a foreigner, the land God gave to Abraham." ⁵ So Isaac sent Jacob to Paddan-aram, to Laban son of Bethuel the Aramean, the brother of Rebekah, the mother of Jacob and Esau.

HEBREWS 12:14–17

¹⁴ Pursue peace with everyone, and holiness—without it no one will see the Lord. ¹⁵ Make sure that no one falls short of the grace of God and that no root of bitterness springs up, causing trouble and defiling many. ¹⁶ And make sure that there isn't any immoral or irreverent person like Esau, who sold his birthright in exchange for a single meal. ¹⁷ For you know that later, when he wanted to inherit the blessing, he was rejected, even though he sought it with tears, because he didn't find any opportunity for repentance.

1   Summarize the events of
    this story.

2   What stood out to you?
    What questions do you have?

3   What is God teaching you
    in the reading?

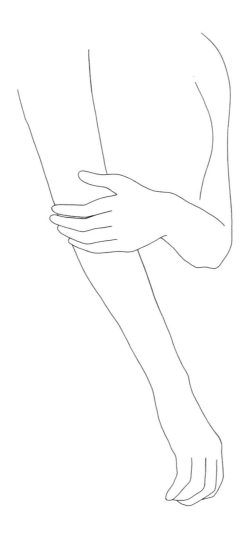

Leah

The Mother of Many Tribes

JACOB MEETS RACHEL

¹ Jacob resumed his journey and went to the eastern country. ² He looked and saw a well in a field. Three flocks of sheep were lying there beside it because the sheep were watered from this well. But a large stone covered the opening of the well. ³ The shepherds would roll the stone from the opening of the well and water the sheep when all the flocks were gathered there. Then they would return the stone to its place over the well's opening.

⁴ Jacob asked the men at the well, "My brothers! Where are you from?"

"We're from Haran," they answered.

⁵ "Do you know Laban grandson of Nahor?" Jacob asked them.

They answered, "We know him."

⁶ "Is he well?" Jacob asked.

"Yes," they said, "and here is his daughter Rachel, coming with his sheep."

⁷ Then Jacob said, "Look, it is still broad daylight. It's not time for the animals to be gathered. Water the flock, then go out and let them graze."

⁸ But they replied, "We can't until all the flocks have been gathered and the stone is rolled from the well's opening. Then we will water the sheep."

⁹ While he was still speaking with them, Rachel came with her father's sheep, for she was a shepherdess. ¹⁰ As soon as Jacob saw his uncle Laban's daughter Rachel with his sheep, he went up and rolled the stone from the opening and watered his uncle Laban's sheep. ¹¹ Then Jacob kissed Rachel and wept loudly. ¹² He told Rachel that he was her father's relative, Rebekah's son. She ran and told her father.

JACOB DECEIVED

¹³ When Laban heard the news about his sister's son Jacob, he ran to meet him, hugged him, and kissed him. Then he took him to his house, and Jacob told him all that had happened.

¹⁴ Laban said to him, "Yes, you are my own flesh and blood."

After Jacob had stayed with him a month, ¹⁵ Laban said to him, "Just because you're my relative, should you work for me for nothing? Tell me what your wages should be."

¹⁶ Now Laban had two daughters: the older was named Leah, and the younger was named Rachel. ¹⁷ Leah had tender eyes, but Rachel was shapely and beautiful. ¹⁸ Jacob loved Rachel, so he answered Laban, "I'll work for you seven years for your younger daughter Rachel."

¹⁹ Laban replied, "Better that I give her to you than to some other man. Stay with me." ²⁰ So Jacob worked seven years for Rachel, and they seemed like only a few days to him because of his love for her.

²¹ Then Jacob said to Laban, "Since my time is complete, give me my wife, so I can sleep with her." ²² So Laban invited all the men of the place and sponsored a feast. ²³ That evening, Laban took his daughter Leah and gave her to Jacob, and he slept with her. ²⁴ And Laban gave his slave Zilpah to his daughter Leah as her slave.

²⁵ When morning came, there was Leah! So he said to Laban, "What is this you have done to me? Wasn't it for Rachel that I worked for you? Why have you deceived me?"

²⁶ Laban answered, "It is not the custom in this place to give the younger daughter in marriage before the firstborn. ²⁷ Complete this week of wedding celebration, and we will also give you this younger one in return for working yet another seven years for me."

²⁸ And Jacob did just that. He finished the week of celebration, and Laban gave him his daughter Rachel as his wife. ²⁹ And Laban gave his slave Bilhah to his daughter Rachel as her slave. ³⁰ Jacob slept with Rachel also, and indeed, he loved Rachel more than Leah. And he worked for Laban another seven years.

[31] When the Lord saw that Leah was unloved, he opened her womb; but Rachel was unable to conceive. [32] Leah conceived, gave birth to a son, and named him Reuben, for she said, "The Lord has seen my affliction; surely my husband will love me now."

[33] She conceived again, gave birth to a son, and said, "The Lord heard that I am unloved and has given me this son also." So she named him Simeon.

[34] She conceived again, gave birth to a son, and said, "At last, my husband will become attached to me because I have borne three sons for him." Therefore he was named Levi.

[35] And she conceived again, gave birth to a son, and said, "This time I will praise the Lord." Therefore she named him Judah. Then Leah stopped having children.

PSALM 63:1–4
PRAISE GOD WHO SATISFIES

A psalm of David. When he was in the Wilderness of Judah.

[1] God, you are my God; I eagerly seek you.
I thirst for you;
my body faints for you
in a land that is dry, desolate, and without water.
[2] So I gaze on you in the sanctuary
to see your strength and your glory.

[3] My lips will glorify you
because your faithful love is better than life.
[4] So I will bless you as long as I live;
at your name, I will lift up my hands.

MATTHEW 1:1–16
THE GENEALOGY OF JESUS CHRIST

[1] An account of the genealogy of Jesus Christ, the Son of David, the Son of Abraham:

FROM ABRAHAM TO DAVID

[2] Abraham fathered Isaac,
Isaac fathered Jacob,
Jacob fathered Judah and his brothers,
[3] Judah fathered Perez and Zerah by Tamar,
Perez fathered Hezron,
Hezron fathered Aram,
[4] Aram fathered Amminadab,
Amminadab fathered Nahshon,
Nahshon fathered Salmon,
[5] Salmon fathered Boaz by Rahab,
Boaz fathered Obed by Ruth,
Obed fathered Jesse,
[6] and Jesse fathered King David.

FROM DAVID TO THE BABYLONIAN EXILE

David fathered Solomon by Uriah's wife,
[7] Solomon fathered Rehoboam,
Rehoboam fathered Abijah,
Abijah fathered Asa,
[8] Asa fathered Jehoshaphat,
Jehoshaphat fathered Joram,
Joram fathered Uzziah,
[9] Uzziah fathered Jotham,
Jotham fathered Ahaz,
Ahaz fathered Hezekiah,
[10] Hezekiah fathered Manasseh,
Manasseh fathered Amon,
Amon fathered Josiah,
[11] and Josiah fathered Jeconiah and his brothers
at the time of the exile to Babylon.

FROM THE EXILE TO THE CHRIST

[12] After the exile to Babylon
Jeconiah fathered Shealtiel,
Shealtiel fathered Zerubbabel,
[13] Zerubbabel fathered Abiud,
Abiud fathered Eliakim,
Eliakim fathered Azor,
[14] Azor fathered Zadok,
Zadok fathered Achim,
Achim fathered Eliud,
[15] Eliud fathered Eleazar,
Eleazar fathered Matthan,
Matthan fathered Jacob,
[16] and Jacob fathered Joseph the husband of Mary,
who gave birth to Jesus who is called the Christ.

1 | Summarize the events of
this story.

2 | What stood out to you?
What questions do you have?

3 | What is God teaching you
in the reading?

Rachel

The Barren Wife Remembered by God

¹ When Rachel saw that she was not bearing Jacob any children, she envied her sister. "Give me sons, or I will die!" she said to Jacob.

² Jacob became angry with Rachel and said, "Am I in God's place, who has withheld offspring from you?"

³ Then she said, "Here is my maid Bilhah. Go sleep with her, and she'll bear children for me so that through her I too can build a family." ⁴ So Rachel gave her slave Bilhah to Jacob as a wife, and he slept with her. ⁵ Bilhah conceived and bore Jacob a son. ⁶ Rachel said, "God has vindicated me; yes, he has heard me and given me a son," so she named him Dan.

⁷ Rachel's slave Bilhah conceived again and bore Jacob a second son. ⁸ Rachel said, "In my wrestlings with God, I have wrestled with my sister and won," and she named him Naphtali.

⁹ When Leah saw that she had stopped having children, she took her slave Zilpah and gave her to Jacob as a wife. ¹⁰ Leah's slave Zilpah bore Jacob a son. ¹¹ Then Leah said, "What good fortune!" and she named him Gad.

¹² When Leah's slave Zilpah bore Jacob a second son, ¹³ Leah said, "I am happy that the women call me happy," so she named him Asher.

¹⁴ Reuben went out during the wheat harvest and found some mandrakes in the field. When he brought them to his mother Leah, Rachel asked, "Please give me some of your son's mandrakes."

¹⁵ But Leah replied to her, "Isn't it enough that you have taken my husband? Now you also want to take my son's mandrakes?"

"Well then," Rachel said, "he can sleep with you tonight in exchange for your son's mandrakes."

¹⁶ When Jacob came in from the field that evening, Leah went out to meet him and said, "You must come with me, for I have hired you with my son's mandrakes." So Jacob slept with her that night.

¹⁷ God listened to Leah, and she conceived and bore Jacob a fifth son. ¹⁸ Leah said, "God has rewarded me for giving my slave to my husband," and she named him Issachar.

¹⁹ Then Leah conceived again and bore Jacob a sixth son. ²⁰ "God has given me a good gift," Leah said. "This time my husband will honor me because I have borne

six sons for him," and she named him Zebulun. ²¹ Later, Leah bore a daughter and named her Dinah.

²² Then God remembered Rachel. He listened to her and opened her womb. ²³ She conceived and bore a son, and she said, "God has taken away my disgrace." ²⁴ She named him Joseph and said, "May the Lord add another son to me."

GENESIS 35:16–20
RACHEL'S DEATH

¹⁶ They set out from Bethel. When they were still some distance from Ephrath, Rachel began to give birth, and her labor was difficult. ¹⁷ During her difficult labor, the midwife said to her, "Don't be afraid, for you have another son." ¹⁸ With her last breath—for she was dying—she named him Ben-oni, but his father called him Benjamin. ¹⁹ So Rachel died and was buried on the way to Ephrath (that is, Bethlehem). ²⁰ Jacob set up a marker on her grave; it is the marker at Rachel's grave still today.

PSALM 98:1–3
PRAISE THE KING

A psalm.

¹ Sing a new song to the Lord,
for he has performed wonders;
his right hand and holy arm
have won him victory.
² The Lord has made his victory known;
he has revealed his righteousness
in the sight of the nations.
³ He has remembered his love
and faithfulness to the house of Israel;
all the ends of the earth
have seen our God's victory.

HEBREWS 4:16

Therefore, let us approach the throne of grace with boldness, so that we may receive mercy and find grace to help us in time of need.

1   Summarize the events of
    this story.

2   What stood out to you?
    What questions do you have?

3   What is God teaching you
    in the reading?

Ricotta French Toast

PREP TIME	COOK TIME	TOTAL TIME	SERVINGS
10 minutes	20 minutes	30 minutes	2

HAYLIE ABELE

@ourbalancedbowl

INGREDIENTS

RICOTTA FRENCH TOAST

1 cup whole milk

½ cup whole milk ricotta cheese, divided

2 eggs

½ tablespoon cinnamon

2 tablespoons white sugar

1 teaspoon vanilla extract

2–3 tablespoons butter

4 slices thick, high quality bread

Maple syrup (optional)

BLACKBERRY COMPOTE

1 pint blackberries (save a few for garnish!)

¼ cup sugar

1 lemon, juiced

¼ cup water

Cornstarch

DIRECTIONS

In a large bowl that you can dip bread in, mix whole milk, ¼ cup of the ricotta cheese, eggs, cinnamon, vanilla extract, and white sugar together until fully combined. Set aside.

For the blackberry compote, add blackberries, sugar, lemon juice, and water to a small pot. Cook on low–medium heat until the blackberries begin to extract their juices and compote thickens slightly. Use a small amount of cornstarch, if needed, to help thicken. Remove from heat while you make the french toast.

In a large non-stick pan, melt a tablespoon of butter over medium heat. Once melted, dip one slice of bread at a time into the french toast mixture on both sides. Place in the pan. Fry on first side for 2 to 3 minutes, or until golden brown. Flip and repeat.

Once the french toast is finished, add blackberry compote, a spoonful of ricotta cheese, and maple syrup, if desired. Eat while warm!

Grace Day

Use this day to pray, rest, and reflect on this week's reading,
giving thanks for the grace that is ours in Christ.

HEBREWS 12:14

Pursue peace with everyone,
and holiness—without it no
one will see the Lord.

Scripture is God-breathed and true. When we memorize it, we carry the gospel with us wherever we go.

This week we'll memorize a verse we read together after Leah's story on day 12. Written by David, Psalm 63:1 is an encouragement to us that we can cry out to God in every circumstance.

Weekly Truth

God, you are my God; I eagerly seek you. I thirst for you; my body faints for you in a land that is dry, desolate, and without water.

Find the corresponding memory card in the back of this book.

Jacob

The Man Who Wrestled with God

GENESIS 28:10–22
JACOB AT BETHEL

¹⁰ Jacob left Beer-sheba and went toward Haran. ¹¹ He reached a certain place and spent the night there because the sun had set. He took one of the stones from the place, put it there at his head, and lay down in that place. ¹² And he dreamed: A stairway was set on the ground with its top reaching the sky, and God's angels were going up and down on it. ¹³ The LORD was standing there beside him, saying, "I am the LORD, the God of your father Abraham and the God of Isaac. I will give you and your offspring the land on which you are lying. ¹⁴ Your offspring will be like the dust of the earth, and you will spread out toward the west, the east, the north, and the south. All the peoples on earth will be blessed through you and your offspring. ¹⁵ Look, I am with you and will watch over you wherever you go. I will bring you back to this land, for I will not leave you until I have done what I have promised you."

¹⁶ When Jacob awoke from his sleep, he said, "Surely the LORD is in this place, and I did not know it." ¹⁷ He was afraid and said, "What an awesome place this is! This is none other than the house of God. This is the gate of heaven."

¹⁸ Early in the morning Jacob took the stone that was near his head and set it up as a marker. He poured oil on top of it ¹⁹ and named the place Bethel, though previously the city was named Luz. ²⁰ Then Jacob made a vow: "If God will be with me and watch over me during this journey I'm making,

if he provides me with food to eat and clothing to wear, ²¹ and if I return safely to my father's family, then the LORD will be my God. ²² This stone that I have set up as a marker will be God's house, and I will give to you a tenth of all that you give me."

GENESIS 31:13

"I am the God of Bethel, where you poured oil on the stone marker and made a solemn vow to me. Get up, leave this land, and return to your native land."

GENESIS 32:3–32

³ Jacob sent messengers ahead of him to his brother Esau in the land of Seir, the territory of Edom. ⁴ He commanded them, "You are to say to my lord Esau, 'This is what your servant Jacob says. I have been staying with Laban and have been delayed until now. ⁵ I have oxen, donkeys, flocks, and male and female slaves. I have sent this message to inform my lord, in order to seek your favor.'"

⁶ When the messengers returned to Jacob, they said, "We went to your brother Esau; he is coming to meet you—and he has four hundred men with him." ⁷ Jacob was greatly afraid and distressed; he divided the people with him into two camps, along with the flocks, herds, and camels.

8 He thought, "If Esau comes to one camp and attacks it, the remaining one can escape."

9 Then Jacob said, "God of my father Abraham and God of my father Isaac, the LORD who said to me, 'Go back to your land and to your family, and I will cause you to prosper,' 10 I am unworthy of all the kindness and faithfulness you have shown your servant. Indeed, I crossed over the Jordan with my staff, and now I have become two camps. 11 Please rescue me from my brother Esau, for I am afraid of him; otherwise, he may come and attack me, the mothers, and their children. 12 You have said, 'I will cause you to prosper, and I will make your offspring like the sand of the sea, too numerous to be counted.'"

13 He spent the night there and took part of what he had brought with him as a gift for his brother Esau: 14 two hundred female goats, twenty male goats, two hundred ewes, twenty rams, 15 thirty milk camels with their young, forty cows, ten bulls, twenty female donkeys, and ten male donkeys. 16 He entrusted them to his slaves as separate herds and said to them, "Go on ahead of me, and leave some distance between the herds."

17 And he told the first one: "When my brother Esau meets you and asks, 'Who do you belong to? Where are you going? And whose animals are these ahead of you?' 18 then tell him, 'They belong to your servant Jacob. They are a gift sent to my lord Esau. And look, he is behind us.'"

19 He also told the second one, the third, and everyone who was walking behind the animals, "Say the same thing to Esau when you find him. 20 You are also to say, 'Look, your servant Jacob is right behind us.'" For he thought, "I want to appease Esau with the gift that is going ahead of me. After that, I can face him, and perhaps he will forgive me."

21 So the gift was sent on ahead of him while he remained in the camp that night. 22 During the night Jacob got up and took his two wives, his two slave women, and his eleven sons, and crossed the ford of Jabbok. 23 He took them and sent them across the stream, along with all his possessions.

JACOB WRESTLES WITH GOD

24 Jacob was left alone, and a man wrestled with him until daybreak. 25 When the man saw that he could not defeat him, he struck Jacob's hip socket as they wrestled and dislocated his hip. 26 Then he said to Jacob, "Let me go, for it is daybreak."

But Jacob said, "I will not let you go unless you bless me."

27 "What is your name?" the man asked.

"Jacob," he replied.

28 "Your name will no longer be Jacob," he said. "It will be Israel because you have struggled with God and with men and have prevailed."

29 Then Jacob asked him, "Please tell me your name."

But he answered, "Why do you ask my name?" And he blessed him there.

30 Jacob then named the place Peniel, "For I have seen God face to face," he said, "yet my life has been spared." 31 The sun shone on him as he passed by Penuel—limping because of his hip. 32 That is why, still today, the Israelites don't eat the thigh muscle that is at the hip socket: because he struck Jacob's hip socket at the thigh muscle.

GENESIS 33:1–11
JACOB MEETS ESAU

1 Now Jacob looked up and saw Esau coming toward him with four hundred men. So he divided the children among Leah, Rachel, and the two slave women. 2 He put the slaves and their children first, Leah and her children next, and Rachel and Joseph last. 3 He himself went on ahead and bowed to the ground seven times until he approached his brother.

4 But Esau ran to meet him, hugged him, threw his arms around him, and kissed him. Then they wept. 5 When Esau looked up and saw the women and children, he asked, "Who are these with you?"

He answered, "The children God has graciously given your servant." ⁶ Then the slaves and their children approached him and bowed down. ⁷ Leah and her children also approached and bowed down, and then Joseph and Rachel approached and bowed down.

⁸ So Esau said, "What do you mean by this whole procession I met?"

"To find favor with you, my lord," he answered.

⁹ "I have enough, my brother," Esau replied. "Keep what you have."

¹⁰ But Jacob said, "No, please! If I have found favor with you, take this gift from me. For indeed, I have seen your face, and it is like seeing God's face, since you have accepted me. ¹¹ Please take my present that was brought to you, because God has been gracious to me and I have everything I need." So Jacob urged him until he accepted.

GENESIS 35:9-15

⁹ God appeared to Jacob again after he returned from Paddan-aram, and he blessed him. ¹⁰ God said to him, "Your name is Jacob; you will no longer be named Jacob, but your name will be Israel." So he named him Israel. ¹¹ God also said to him, "I am God Almighty. Be fruitful and multiply. A nation, indeed an assembly of nations, will come from you, and kings will descend from you. ¹² I will give to you the land that I gave to Abraham and Isaac. And I will give the land to your future descendants." ¹³ Then God withdrew from him at the place where he had spoken to him.

¹⁴ Jacob set up a marker at the place where he had spoken to him—a stone marker. He poured a drink offering on it and anointed it with oil. ¹⁵ Jacob named the place where God had spoken with him Bethel.

JOHN 1:43-51
PHILIP AND NATHANAEL

⁴³ The next day Jesus decided to leave for Galilee. He found Philip and told him, "Follow me."

⁴⁴ Now Philip was from Bethsaida, the hometown of Andrew and Peter. ⁴⁵ Philip found Nathanael and told him, "We have found the one Moses wrote about in the law (and so did the prophets): Jesus the son of Joseph, from Nazareth."

⁴⁶ "Can anything good come out of Nazareth?" Nathanael asked him.

"Come and see," Philip answered.

⁴⁷ Then Jesus saw Nathanael coming toward him and said about him, "Here truly is an Israelite in whom there is no deceit."

⁴⁸ "How do you know me?" Nathanael asked.

"Before Philip called you, when you were under the fig tree, I saw you," Jesus answered.

⁴⁹ "Rabbi," Nathanael replied, "You are the Son of God; you are the King of Israel!"

⁵⁰ Jesus responded to him, "Do you believe because I told you I saw you under the fig tree? You will see greater things than this." ⁵¹ Then he said, "Truly I tell you, you will see heaven opened and the angels of God ascending and descending on the Son of Man."

1 Summarize the events of
   this story.

2 What stood out to you?
   What questions do you have?

3 What is God teaching you
   in the reading?

Joseph

The Slave Preserved and Promoted by the Lord

GENESIS 37:1–13, 18–28
JOSEPH'S DREAMS

¹ Jacob lived in the land where his father had stayed, the land of Canaan. ² These are the family records of Jacob.

At seventeen years of age, Joseph tended sheep with his brothers. The young man was working with the sons of Bilhah and Zilpah, his father's wives, and he brought a bad report about them to their father.

³ Now Israel loved Joseph more than his other sons because Joseph was a son born to him in his old age, and he made a robe of many colors for him. ⁴ When his brothers saw that their father loved him more than all his brothers, they hated him and could not bring themselves to speak peaceably to him.

⁵ Then Joseph had a dream. When he told it to his brothers, they hated him even more. ⁶ He said to them, "Listen to this dream I had: ⁷ There we were, binding sheaves of grain in the field. Suddenly my sheaf stood up, and your sheaves gathered around it and bowed down to my sheaf."

⁸ "Are you really going to reign over us?" his brothers asked him. "Are you really going to rule us?" So they hated him even more because of his dream and what he had said.

⁹ Then he had another dream and told it to his brothers. "Look," he said, "I had another dream, and this time the sun, moon, and eleven stars were bowing down to me."

¹⁰ He told his father and brothers, and his father rebuked him. "What kind of dream is this that you have had?" he said. "Am I and your mother and your brothers really going to come and bow down to the ground before you?" ¹¹ His brothers were jealous of him, but his father kept the matter in mind.

JOSEPH SOLD INTO SLAVERY

¹² His brothers had gone to pasture their father's flocks at Shechem. ¹³ Israel said to Joseph, "Your brothers, you know, are pasturing the flocks at Shechem. Get ready. I'm sending you to them."

"I'm ready," Joseph replied.

…

¹⁸ They saw him in the distance, and before he had reached them, they plotted to kill him. ¹⁹ They said to one another, "Oh, look, here comes that dream expert! ²⁰ So now, come on, let's kill him and throw him into one of the pits. We can say that a vicious animal ate him. Then we'll see what becomes of his dreams!"

²¹ When Reuben heard this, he tried to save him from them. He said, "Let's not take his life." ²² Reuben also said to them, "Don't shed blood. Throw him into this pit in the wilderness, but don't lay a hand on him"—intending to rescue him from them and return him to his father.

²³ When Joseph came to his brothers, they stripped off Joseph's robe, the robe of many colors that he had on. ²⁴ Then they took him and threw him into the pit. The pit was empty, without water.

²⁵ They sat down to eat a meal, and when they looked up, there was a caravan of Ishmaelites coming from Gilead. Their camels were carrying aromatic gum, balsam, and resin, going down to Egypt.

²⁶ Judah said to his brothers, "What do we gain if we kill our brother and cover up his blood? ²⁷ Come on, let's sell him to the Ishmaelites and not lay a hand on him, for he is our brother, our own flesh," and his brothers agreed. ²⁸ When Midianite traders passed by, his brothers pulled Joseph out of the pit and sold him for twenty pieces of silver to the Ishmaelites, who took Joseph to Egypt.

ACTS 7:9–16

THE PATRIARCHS IN EGYPT

⁹ The patriarchs became jealous of Joseph and sold him into Egypt, but God was with him ¹⁰ and rescued him out of all his troubles. He gave him favor and wisdom in the sight of Pharaoh, king of Egypt, who appointed him ruler over Egypt and over his whole household. ¹¹ Now a famine and great suffering came over all of

Egypt and Canaan, and our ancestors could find no food. [12] When Jacob heard there was grain in Egypt, he sent our ancestors there the first time. [13] The second time, Joseph revealed himself to his brothers, and Joseph's family became known to Pharaoh. [14] Joseph invited his father Jacob and all his relatives, seventy-five people in all, [15] and Jacob went down to Egypt. He and our ancestors died there, [16] were carried back to Shechem, and were placed in the tomb that Abraham had bought for a sum of silver from the sons of Hamor in Shechem.

GENESIS 50:20

You planned evil against me; God planned it for good to bring about the present result—the survival of many people.

GENESIS 50:15–21

JOSEPH'S KINDNESS

[15] When Joseph's brothers saw that their father was dead, they said to one another, "If Joseph is holding a grudge against us, he will certainly repay us for all the suffering we caused him."

[16] So they sent this message to Joseph, "Before he died your father gave a command: [17] 'Say this to Joseph: Please forgive your brothers' transgression and their sin— the suffering they caused you.' Therefore, please forgive the transgression of the servants of the God of your father." Joseph wept when their message came to him. [18] His brothers also came to him, bowed down before him, and said, "We are your slaves!"

[19] But Joseph said to them, "Don't be afraid. Am I in the place of God? [20] You planned evil against me; God planned it for good to bring about the present result—the survival of many people. [21] Therefore don't be afraid. I will take care of you and your children." And he comforted them and spoke kindly to them.

1 Summarize the events of
   this story.

2 What stood out to you?
   What questions do you have?

3 What is God teaching you
   in the reading?

Potiphar's Wife

A Woman of Unrequited Advances and Unflinching Lies

GENESIS 39

JOSEPH IN POTIPHAR'S HOUSE

[1] Now Joseph had been taken to Egypt. An Egyptian named Potiphar, an officer of Pharaoh and the captain of the guards, bought him from the Ishmaelites who had brought him there. [2] The LORD was with Joseph, and he became a successful man, serving in the household of his Egyptian master. [3] When his master saw that the LORD was with him and that the LORD made everything he did successful, [4] Joseph found favor with his master and became his personal attendant. Potiphar also put him in charge of his household and placed all that he owned under his authority. [5] From the time that he put him in charge of his household and of all that he owned, the LORD blessed the Egyptian's house because of Joseph. The LORD's blessing was on all that he owned, in his house and in his fields. [6] He left all that he owned under Joseph's authority; he did not concern himself with anything except the food he ate.

Now Joseph was well-built and handsome. [7] After some time his master's wife looked longingly at Joseph and said, "Sleep with me."

[8] But he refused. "Look," he said to his master's wife, "with me here my master does not concern himself with anything in his house, and he has put all that he owns under my authority. [9] No one in this house is greater than I am. He has withheld nothing from me except you, because you are his wife. So how could I do this immense evil, and how could I sin against God?"

[10] Although she spoke to Joseph day after day, he refused to go to bed with her. [11] Now one day he went into the house to do his work, and none of the household servants were there. [12] She grabbed him by his garment and said, "Sleep with me!" But leaving his garment in her hand, he escaped and ran outside. [13] When she saw that he had left his garment with her and had run outside, [14] she called her household servants. "Look," she said to them, "my husband brought a Hebrew man to make fools of us. He came to me so he could sleep with me, and I screamed as loud as I could. [15] When he heard me screaming for help, he left his garment beside me and ran outside."

[16] She put Joseph's garment beside her until his master came home. [17] Then she told him the same story: "The Hebrew slave you brought to us came to make a fool of me, [18] but when I screamed for help, he left his garment beside me and ran outside."

[19] When his master heard the story his wife told him—"These are the things your slave did to me"—he was furious [20] and had him thrown into prison, where the king's prisoners were confined. So Joseph was there in prison.

JOSEPH IN PRISON

[21] But the LORD was with Joseph and extended kindness to him. He granted him favor with the prison warden. [22] The warden put all the prisoners who were in the prison under Joseph's authority, and he was responsible for everything that was done there. [23] The warden did not bother with anything under Joseph's authority, because the LORD was with him, and the LORD made everything that he did successful.

PROVERBS 24:15–16

[15] Don't set an ambush, you wicked one,
at the camp of the righteous man;
don't destroy his dwelling.
[16] Though a righteous person falls seven times,
he will get up,
but the wicked will stumble into ruin.

EPHESIANS 5:1–4

[1] Therefore, be imitators of God, as dearly loved children, [2] and walk in love, as Christ also loved us and gave himself for us, a sacrificial and fragrant offering to God. [3] But sexual immorality and any impurity or greed should not even be heard of among you, as is proper for saints. [4] Obscene and foolish talking or crude joking are not suitable, but rather giving thanks.

For God has not called us to impurity but to live in holiness.

---

1 THESSALONIANS 4:1–8
THE CALL TO SANCTIFICATION

[1] Additionally then, brothers and sisters, we ask and encourage you in the Lord Jesus, that as you have received instruction from us on how you should live and please God—as you are doing—do this even more. [2] For you know what commands we gave you through the Lord Jesus.

[3] For this is God's will, your sanctification: that you keep away from sexual immorality, [4] that each of you knows how to control his own body in holiness and honor, [5] not with lustful passions, like the Gentiles, who don't know God. [6] This means one must not transgress against and take advantage of a brother or sister in this manner, because the Lord is an avenger of all these offenses, as we also previously told and warned you. [7] For God has not called us to impurity but to live in holiness. [8] Consequently, anyone who rejects this does not reject man, but God, who gives you his Holy Spirit.

1   Summarize the events of
    this story.

2   What stood out to you?
    What questions do you have?

3   What is God teaching you
    in the reading?

Shiphrah and Puah

Egyptian Midwives Who Feared the Lord

EXODUS 1:8–21

⁸ A new king, who did not know about Joseph, came to power in Egypt. ⁹ He said to his people, "Look, the Israelite people are more numerous and powerful than we are. ¹⁰ Come, let's deal shrewdly with them; otherwise they will multiply further, and when war breaks out, they will join our enemies, fight against us, and leave the country." ¹¹ So the Egyptians assigned taskmasters over the Israelites to oppress them with forced labor. They built Pithom and Rameses as supply cities for Pharaoh. ¹² But the more they oppressed them, the more they multiplied and spread so that the Egyptians came to dread the Israelites. ¹³ They worked the Israelites ruthlessly ¹⁴ and made their lives bitter with difficult labor in brick and mortar and in all kinds of fieldwork. They ruthlessly imposed all this work on them.

¹⁵ The king of Egypt said to the Hebrew midwives—the first whose name was Shiphrah and the second whose name was Puah— ¹⁶ "When you help the Hebrew women give birth, observe them as they deliver. If the child is a son, kill him, but if it's a daughter, she may live." ¹⁷ The midwives, however, feared God and did not do as the king of Egypt had told them; they let the boys live. ¹⁸ So the king of Egypt summoned the midwives and asked them, "Why have you done this and let the boys live?"

¹⁹ The midwives said to Pharaoh, "The Hebrew women are not like the Egyptian women, for they are vigorous and give birth before the midwife can get to them."

²⁰ So God was good to the midwives, and the people multiplied and became very numerous. ²¹ Since the midwives feared God, he gave them families.

PSALM 34

THE LORD DELIVERS THE RIGHTEOUS

Concerning David, when he pretended to be insane in the presence of Abimelech, who drove him out, and he departed.

¹ I will bless the LORD at all times;
his praise will always be on my lips.
² I will boast in the LORD;
the humble will hear and be glad.
³ Proclaim the LORD's greatness with me;
let us exalt his name together.

⁴ I sought the LORD, and he answered me
and rescued me from all my fears.
⁵ Those who look to him are radiant with joy;
their faces will never be ashamed.
⁶ This poor man cried, and the LORD heard him
and saved him from all his troubles.
⁷ The angel of the LORD encamps
around those who fear him, and rescues them.

⁸ Taste and see that the LORD is good.
How happy is the person who takes refuge in him!

The midwives, however, feared God and did not do as the king of Egypt had told them.

———

⁹ You who are his holy ones, fear the LORD,
for those who fear him lack nothing.
¹⁰ Young lions lack food and go hungry,
but those who seek the LORD
will not lack any good thing.

¹¹ Come, children, listen to me;
I will teach you the fear of the LORD.
¹² Who is someone who desires life,
loving a long life to enjoy what is good?
¹³ Keep your tongue from evil
and your lips from deceitful speech.
¹⁴ Turn away from evil and do what is good;
seek peace and pursue it.

¹⁵ The eyes of the LORD are on the righteous,
and his ears are open to their cry for help.
¹⁶ The face of the LORD is set
against those who do what is evil,
to remove all memory of them from the earth.
¹⁷ The righteous cry out, and the LORD hears,
and rescues them from all their troubles.
¹⁸ The LORD is near the brokenhearted;
he saves those crushed in spirit.

¹⁹ One who is righteous has many adversities,
but the LORD rescues him from them all.
²⁰ He protects all his bones;
not one of them is broken.
²¹ Evil brings death to the wicked,
and those who hate the righteous will be punished.
²² The LORD redeems the life of his servants,
and all who take refuge in him will not be punished.

GALATIANS 6:7–10

⁷ Don't be deceived: God is not mocked. For whatever a person sows he will also reap, ⁸ because the one who sows to his flesh will reap destruction from the flesh, but the one who sows to the Spirit will reap eternal life from the Spirit. ⁹ Let us not get tired of doing good, for we will reap at the proper time if we don't give up. ¹⁰ Therefore, as we have opportunity, let us work for the good of all, especially for those who belong to the household of faith.

1 Summarize the events of
this story.

2 What stood out to you?
What questions do you have?

3 What is God teaching you
in the reading?

Moses

The Man Who Led God's People Out of Slavery

ACTS 7:17–36

[17] As the time was approaching to fulfill the promise that God had made to Abraham, the people flourished and multiplied in Egypt [18] until a different king who did not know Joseph ruled over Egypt. [19] He dealt deceitfully with our race and oppressed our ancestors by making them abandon their infants outside so that they wouldn't survive. [20] At this time Moses was born, and he was beautiful in God's sight. He was cared for in his father's home for three months. [21] When he was put outside, Pharaoh's daughter adopted and raised him as her own son. [22] So Moses was educated in all the wisdom of the Egyptians and was powerful in his speech and actions.

[23] When he was forty years old, he decided to visit his own people, the Israelites. [24] When he saw one of them being mistreated, he came to his rescue and avenged the oppressed man by striking down the Egyptian. [25] He assumed his people would understand that God would give them deliverance through him, but they did not understand. [26] The next day he showed up while they were fighting and tried to reconcile them peacefully, saying, "Men, you are brothers. Why are you mistreating each other?"

[27] But the one who was mistreating his neighbor pushed Moses aside, saying: Who appointed you a ruler and a judge over us? [28] Do you want to kill me, the same way you killed the Egyptian yesterday?

[29] When he heard this, Moses fled and became an exile in the land of Midian, where he became the father of two sons. [30] After forty years had passed, an angel appeared to him in the wilderness of Mount Sinai, in the flame of a burning bush. [31] When Moses saw it, he was amazed at the sight. As he was approaching to look at it, the voice of the Lord came: [32] I am the God of your ancestors—the God of Abraham, of Isaac, and of Jacob. Moses began to tremble and did not dare to look.

[33] The Lord said to him: Take off the sandals from your feet, because the place where you are standing is holy ground. [34] I have certainly seen the oppression of my people in Egypt; I have heard their groaning and have come down to set them free. And now, come, I will send you to Egypt.

[35] This Moses, whom they rejected when they said, Who appointed you a ruler and a judge?—this one God sent as a ruler and a deliverer through the angel who appeared to him in the bush. [36] This man led them out and performed wonders and signs in the land of Egypt, at the Red Sea, and in the wilderness for forty years.

EXODUS 3:1–22

MOSES AND THE BURNING BUSH

¹ Meanwhile, Moses was shepherding the flock of his father-in-law Jethro, the priest of Midian. He led the flock to the far side of the wilderness and came to Horeb, the mountain of God. ² Then the angel of the LORD appeared to him in a flame of fire within a bush. As Moses looked, he saw that the bush was on fire but was not consumed. ³ So Moses thought, "I must go over and look at this remarkable sight. Why isn't the bush burning up?"

⁴ When the LORD saw that he had gone over to look, God called out to him from the bush, "Moses, Moses!"

"Here I am," he answered.

⁵ "Do not come closer," he said. "Remove the sandals from your feet, for the place where you are standing is holy ground." ⁶ Then he continued, "I am the God of your father, the God of Abraham, the God of Isaac, and the God of Jacob." Moses hid his face because he was afraid to look at God.

⁷ Then the LORD said, "I have observed the misery of my people in Egypt, and have heard them crying out because of their oppressors. I know about their sufferings, ⁸ and I have come down to rescue them from the power of the Egyptians and to bring them from that land to a good and spacious land, a land flowing with milk and honey—the territory of the Canaanites, Hethites, Amorites, Perizzites, Hivites, and Jebusites. ⁹ So because the Israelites' cry for help has come to me, and I have also seen the way the Egyptians are oppressing them, ¹⁰ therefore, go. I am sending you to Pharaoh so that you may lead my people, the Israelites, out of Egypt."

¹¹ But Moses asked God, "Who am I that I should go to Pharaoh and that I should bring the Israelites out of Egypt?"

¹² He answered, "I will certainly be with you, and this will be the sign to you that I am the one who sent you: when you bring the people out of Egypt, you will all worship God at this mountain."

¹³ Then Moses asked God, "If I go to the Israelites and say to them, 'The God of your fathers has sent me to you,' and they ask me, 'What is his name?' what should I tell them?"

¹⁴ God replied to Moses, "I AM WHO I AM. This is what you are to say to the Israelites: I AM has sent me to you." ¹⁵ God also said to Moses, "Say this to the Israelites: The LORD, the God of your fathers, the God of Abraham, the God of Isaac, and the God of Jacob, has sent me to you. This is my name forever; this is how I am to be remembered in every generation.

[16] "Go and assemble the elders of Israel and say to them: The Lord, the God of your fathers, the God of Abraham, Isaac, and Jacob, has appeared to me and said: I have paid close attention to you and to what has been done to you in Egypt. [17] And I have promised you that I will bring you up from the misery of Egypt to the land of the Canaanites, Hethites, Amorites, Perizzites, Hivites, and Jebusites—a land flowing with milk and honey. [18] They will listen to what you say. Then you, along with the elders of Israel, must go to the king of Egypt and say to him: The Lord, the God of the Hebrews, has met with us. Now please let us go on a three-day trip into the wilderness so that we may sacrifice to the Lord our God.

[19] "However, I know that the king of Egypt will not allow you to go, even under force from a strong hand. [20] But when I stretch out my hand and strike Egypt with all my miracles that I will perform in it, after that, he will let you go. [21] And I will give these people such favor with the Egyptians that when you go, you will not go empty-handed. [22] Each woman will ask her neighbor and any woman staying in her house for silver and gold jewelry, and clothing, and you will put them on your sons and daughters. So you will plunder the Egyptians."

EXODUS 4:1–17
MIRACULOUS SIGNS FOR MOSES

[1] Moses answered, "What if they won't believe me and will not obey me but say, 'The Lord did not appear to you'?"

[2] The Lord asked him, "What is that in your hand?"

"A staff," he replied.

[3] "Throw it on the ground," he said. So Moses threw it on the ground, it became a snake, and he ran from it. [4] The Lord told Moses, "Stretch out your hand and grab it by the tail." So he stretched out his hand and caught it, and it became a staff in his hand. [5] "This will take place," he continued, "so that they will believe that the Lord, the God of their fathers, the God of Abraham, the God of Isaac, and the God of Jacob, has appeared to you."

[6] In addition the Lord said to him, "Put your hand inside your cloak." So he put his hand inside his cloak, and when he took it out, his hand was diseased, resembling snow. [7] "Put your hand back inside your cloak," he said. So he put his hand back inside his cloak, and when he took it out, it had again become like the rest of his skin. [8] "If they will not believe you and will not respond to the evidence of the first sign, they may believe the evidence of the second sign. [9] And if they don't believe even these two signs or listen to what you say, take some water from the Nile and pour it on the dry ground. The water you take from the Nile will become blood on the ground."

[10] But Moses replied to the Lord, "Please, Lord, I have never been eloquent—either in the past or recently or since you have been speaking to your servant—because my mouth and my tongue are sluggish."

[11] The Lord said to him, "Who placed a mouth on humans? Who makes a person mute or deaf, seeing or blind? Is it not I, the Lord? [12] Now go! I will help you speak and I will teach you what to say."

[13] Moses said, "Please, Lord, send someone else."

[14] Then the Lord's anger burned against Moses, and he said, "Isn't Aaron the Levite your brother? I know that he can speak well. And also, he is on his way now to meet you. He will rejoice when he sees you. [15] You will speak with him and tell him what to say. I will help both you and him to speak and will teach you both what to do. [16] He will speak to the people for you. He will serve as a mouth for you, and you will serve as God to him. [17] And take this staff in your hand that you will perform the signs with."

1   Summarize the events of
    this story.

2   What stood out to you?
    What questions do you have?

3   What is God teaching you
    in the reading?

Roasted Garlic and Lemon Hummus

PREP TIME
10 minutes

SERVINGS
10

TYNIA PEAY
@ontysplate

INGREDIENTS

15 ounces canned chickpeas, drained and rinsed

10 roasted garlic cloves

2 preserved lemons

1 lemon juiced, about 6 tablespoons

⅓ cup olive oil

¼ cup cashew butter

¼ cup water

½ teaspoon kosher salt, to taste

Cayenne and fresh flat leaf parsley, to garnish

INSTRUCTIONS

Combine ingredients in a blender and pulse until smooth. You may choose to add more water for a creamier texture or less for a thicker dip.

Garnish with olive oil, cayenne, and parsley and serve at room temperature or cold with a fresh batch of naan!

Grace Day

Use this day to pray, rest, and reflect on this week's reading,
giving thanks for the grace that is ours in Christ.

Therefore, be imitators of God, as dearly loved children, and walk in love, as Christ also loved us and gave himself for us, a sacrificial and fragrant offering to God.

DAY 21

WEEK 3

Scripture is God-breathed and true. When we memorize it, we carry the gospel with us wherever we go.

On day 18, we read the story of Shiphrah and Puah, Egyptian midwives who feared God and defied the orders of Pharaoh to protect God's people. This week we'll memorize Psalm 34:7, a verse from that day's reading that celebrates God's goodness and power to protect those who seek refuge in Him.

Weekly Truth

PSALM 34:7

The angel of the LORD encamps around those who fear him, and rescues them.

Find the corresponding memory card in the back of this book.

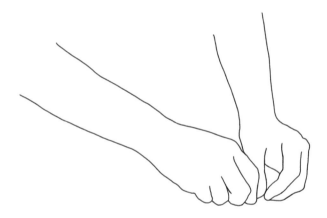

Aaron

The First High Priest

REUNION OF MOSES AND AARON

[27] Now the Lord had said to Aaron, "Go and meet Moses in the wilderness." So he went and met him at the mountain of God and kissed him. [28] Moses told Aaron everything the Lord had sent him to say, and about all the signs he had commanded him to do. [29] Then Moses and Aaron went and assembled all the elders of the Israelites. [30] Aaron repeated everything the Lord had said to Moses and performed the signs before the people. [31] The people believed, and when they heard that the Lord had paid attention to them and that he had seen their misery, they knelt low and worshiped.

EXODUS 7:8–13

[8] The Lord said to Moses and Aaron, [9] "When Pharaoh tells you, 'Perform a miracle,' tell Aaron, 'Take your staff and throw it down before Pharaoh. It will become a serpent.'" [10] So Moses and Aaron went in to Pharaoh and did just as the Lord had commanded. Aaron threw down his staff before Pharaoh and his officials, and it became a serpent. [11] But then Pharaoh called the wise men and sorcerers—the magicians of Egypt, and they also did the same thing by their occult practices. [12] Each one threw down his staff, and it became a serpent. But Aaron's staff swallowed their staffs. [13] However, Pharaoh's heart was hard, and he did not listen to them, as the Lord had said.

EXODUS 32:1–6, 21–24

THE GOLD CALF

[1] When the people saw that Moses delayed in coming down from the mountain, they gathered around Aaron and said to him, "Come, make gods for us who will go before us because this Moses, the man who brought us up from the land of Egypt—we don't know what has happened to him!"

[2] Aaron replied to them, "Take off the gold rings that are on the ears of your wives, your sons, and your daughters and bring them to me." [3] So all the people took off the gold rings that were on their ears and brought them to Aaron. [4] He took the gold from them, fashioned it with an engraving tool, and made it into an image of a calf.

Then they said, "Israel, these are your gods, who brought you up from the land of Egypt!"

[5] When Aaron saw this, he built an altar in front of it and made an announcement: "There will be a festival to the Lord tomorrow." [6] Early the next morning they arose, offered burnt offerings, and presented fellowship offerings. The people sat down to eat and drink, and got up to party.

…

Aaron repeated everything the LORD had said to Moses and performed the signs before the people.

———

²¹ Then Moses asked Aaron, "What did these people do to you that you have led them into such a grave sin?"

²² "Don't be enraged, my lord," Aaron replied. "You yourself know that the people are intent on evil. ²³ They said to me, 'Make gods for us who will go before us because this Moses, the man who brought us up from the land of Egypt—we don't know what has happened to him!' ²⁴ So I said to them, 'Whoever has gold, take it off,' and they gave it to me. When I threw it into the fire, out came this calf!"

LEVITICUS 8:1–5
ORDINATION OF AARON AND HIS SONS

¹ The LORD spoke to Moses: ² "Take Aaron, his sons with him, the garments, the anointing oil, the bull of the sin offering, the two rams, and the basket of unleavened bread, ³ and assemble the whole community at the entrance to the tent of meeting." ⁴ So Moses did as the LORD commanded him, and the community assembled at the entrance to the tent of meeting. ⁵ Moses said to them, "This is what the LORD has commanded to be done."

LEVITICUS 9:1–7
THE PRIESTLY MINISTRY INAUGURATED

¹ On the eighth day Moses summoned Aaron, his sons, and the elders of Israel. ² He said to Aaron, "Take a young bull for a sin offering and a ram for a burnt offering, both without blemish, and present them before the LORD. ³ And tell the Israelites: Take a male goat for a sin offering; a calf and a lamb, male yearlings without blemish, for a burnt offering; ⁴ an ox and a ram for a fellowship offering to sacrifice before the LORD; and a grain offering mixed with oil. For today the LORD is going to appear to you."

⁵ They brought what Moses had commanded to the front of the tent of meeting, and the whole community came forward and stood before the LORD. ⁶ Moses said, "This is what the LORD commanded you to do, that the glory of the LORD may appear to you." ⁷ Then Moses said to Aaron, "Approach the altar and sacrifice your sin offering and your burnt offering; make atonement for yourself and the people. Sacrifice the people's offering and make atonement for them, as the LORD commanded."

1 CORINTHIANS 10:7

Don't become idolaters as some of them were; as it is written, The people sat down to eat and drink, and got up to party.

1   Summarize the events of
    this story.

2   What stood out to you?
    What questions do you have?

3   What is God teaching you
    in the reading?

Miriam

A Prophetess with Praise on Her Lips

EXODUS 2:1–8

MOSES'S BIRTH AND ADOPTION

¹ Now a man from the family of Levi married a Levite woman. ² The woman became pregnant and gave birth to a son; when she saw that he was beautiful, she hid him for three months. ³ But when she could no longer hide him, she got a papyrus basket for him and coated it with asphalt and pitch. She placed the child in it and set it among the reeds by the bank of the Nile. ⁴ Then his sister stood at a distance in order to see what would happen to him.

⁵ Pharaoh's daughter went down to bathe at the Nile while her servant girls walked along the riverbank. She saw the basket among the reeds, sent her slave girl, took it, ⁶ opened it, and saw him, the child—and there he was, a little boy, crying. She felt sorry for him and said, "This is one of the Hebrew boys."

⁷ Then his sister said to Pharaoh's daughter, "Should I go and call a Hebrew woman who is nursing to nurse the boy for you?"

⁸ "Go," Pharaoh's daughter told her. So the girl went and called the boy's mother.

EXODUS 14

¹ Then the LORD spoke to Moses: ² "Tell the Israelites to turn back and camp in front of Pi-hahiroth, between Migdol and the sea; you must camp in front of Baal-zephon, facing it by the sea. ³ Pharaoh will say of the Israelites: They are wandering around the land in confusion; the wilderness has boxed them in. ⁴ I will harden Pharaoh's heart so that he will pursue them. Then I will receive glory by means of Pharaoh and all his army, and the Egyptians will know that I am the LORD." So the Israelites did this.

THE EGYPTIAN PURSUIT

⁵ When the king of Egypt was told that the people had fled, Pharaoh and his officials changed their minds about the people and said: "What have we done? We have released Israel from serving us." ⁶ So he got his chariot ready and took his troops with him; ⁷ he took six hundred of the best chariots and all the rest of the chariots of Egypt, with officers in each one. ⁸ The LORD hardened the heart of Pharaoh king of Egypt, and he pursued the Israelites, who were going out defiantly. ⁹ The Egyptians—all Pharaoh's horses and chariots, his horsemen, and his army—chased after them and caught up with them as they camped by the sea beside Pi-hahiroth, in front of Baal-zephon.

¹⁰ As Pharaoh approached, the Israelites looked up and there were the Egyptians coming after them! The Israelites were terrified and cried out to the LORD for help. ¹¹ They said to Moses: "Is it because there are no graves in Egypt that you have taken us away to die in the wilderness? What have you done to us by bringing

us out of Egypt? 12 Isn't this what we told you in Egypt: Leave us alone so that we may serve the Egyptians? It would have been better for us to serve the Egyptians than to die in the wilderness."

13 But Moses said to the people, "Don't be afraid. Stand firm and see the LORD's salvation that he will accomplish for you today; for the Egyptians you see today, you will never see again. 14 The LORD will fight for you, and you must be quiet."

ESCAPE THROUGH THE RED SEA

15 The LORD said to Moses, "Why are you crying out to me? Tell the Israelites to break camp. 16 As for you, lift up your staff, stretch out your hand over the sea, and divide it so that the Israelites can go through the sea on dry ground. 17 As for me, I am going to harden the hearts of the Egyptians so that they will go in after them, and I will receive glory by means of Pharaoh, all his army, and his chariots and horsemen. 18 The Egyptians will know that I am the LORD when I receive glory through Pharaoh, his chariots, and his horsemen."

19 Then the angel of God, who was going in front of the Israelite forces, moved and went behind them. The pillar of cloud moved from in front of them and stood behind them. 20 It came between the Egyptian and Israelite forces. There was cloud and darkness, it lit up the night, and neither group came near the other all night long.

21 Then Moses stretched out his hand over the sea. The LORD drove the sea back with a powerful east wind all that night and turned the sea into dry land. So the waters were divided, 22 and the Israelites went through the sea on dry ground, with the waters like a wall to them on their right and their left.

23 The Egyptians set out in pursuit—all Pharaoh's horses, his chariots, and his horsemen—and went into the sea after them. 24 During the morning watch, the LORD looked down at the Egyptian forces from the pillar of fire and cloud, and threw the Egyptian forces into confusion. 25 He caused their chariot wheels to swerve and made them drive with difficulty. "Let's get away from Israel," the Egyptians said, "because the LORD is fighting for them against Egypt!"

26 Then the LORD said to Moses, "Stretch out your hand over the sea so that the water may come back on the Egyptians, on their chariots and horsemen." 27 So Moses stretched out his hand over the sea, and at daybreak the sea returned to its normal depth. While the Egyptians were trying to escape from it, the LORD threw them into the sea. 28 The water came back and covered the chariots and horsemen, plus the entire army of Pharaoh that had gone after them into the sea. Not even one of them survived.

29 But the Israelites had walked through the sea on dry ground, with the waters like a wall to them on their right and their left. 30 That day the LORD saved Israel from the power of the Egyptians, and Israel saw the Egyptians dead on the seashore. 31 When Israel saw the great power that the LORD used against the Egyptians, the people feared the LORD and believed in him and in his servant Moses.

EXODUS 15:19–21

19 When Pharaoh's horses with his chariots and horsemen went into the sea, the LORD brought the water of the sea back over them. But the Israelites walked through the sea on dry ground. 20 Then the prophetess Miriam, Aaron's sister, took a tambourine in her hand, and all the women came out following her with tambourines and dancing. 21 Miriam sang to them:

> Sing to the LORD,
> for he is highly exalted;
> he has thrown the horse
> and its rider into the sea.

ISAIAH 12:2

Indeed, God is my salvation;
I will trust him and not be afraid,
for the LORD, the LORD himself,
is my strength and my song.
He has become my salvation.

1   Summarize the events of
    this story.

2   What stood out to you?
    What questions do you have?

3   What is God teaching you
    in the reading?

Bezalel

An Artisan Filled with God's Spirit

EXODUS 31:1–11

GOD'S PROVISION OF THE SKILLED WORKERS

¹ The LORD also spoke to Moses: ² "Look, I have appointed by name Bezalel son of Uri, son of Hur, of the tribe of Judah. ³ I have filled him with God's Spirit, with wisdom, understanding, and ability in every craft ⁴ to design artistic works in gold, silver, and bronze, ⁵ to cut gemstones for mounting, and to carve wood for work in every craft. ⁶ I have also selected Oholiab son of Ahisamach, of the tribe of Dan, to be with him. I have put wisdom in the heart of every skilled artisan in order to make all that I have commanded you: ⁷ the tent of meeting, the ark of the testimony, the mercy seat that is on top of it, and all the other furnishings of the tent— ⁸ the table with its utensils, the pure gold lampstand with all its utensils, the altar of incense, ⁹ the altar of burnt offering with all its utensils, the basin with its stand— ¹⁰ the specially woven garments, both the holy garments for the priest Aaron and the garments for his sons to serve as priests, ¹¹ the anointing oil, and the fragrant incense for the sanctuary. They must make them according to all that I have commanded you."

EXODUS 35

THE SABBATH COMMAND

¹ Moses assembled the entire Israelite community and said to them, "These are the things that the LORD has commanded you to do: ² For six days work is to be done, but on the seventh day you are to have a holy day, a Sabbath of complete rest to the LORD. Anyone who does work on it must be executed. ³ Do not light a fire in any of your homes on the Sabbath day."

BUILDING THE TABERNACLE

⁴ Then Moses said to the entire Israelite community, "This is what the LORD has commanded: ⁵ Take up an offering among you for the LORD. Let everyone

whose heart is willing bring this as the Lord's offering: gold, silver, and bronze; ⁶ blue, purple, and scarlet yarn; fine linen and goat hair; ⁷ ram skins dyed red and fine leather; acacia wood; ⁸ oil for the light; spices for the anointing oil and for the fragrant incense; ⁹ and onyx with gemstones to mount on the ephod and breastpiece.

¹⁰ "Let all the skilled artisans among you come and make everything that the Lord has commanded: ¹¹ the tabernacle—its tent and covering, its clasps and supports, its crossbars, its pillars and bases; ¹² the ark with its poles, the mercy seat, and the curtain for the screen; ¹³ the table with its poles, all its utensils, and the Bread of the Presence; ¹⁴ the lampstand for light with its utensils and lamps as well as the oil for the light; ¹⁵ the altar of incense with its poles; the anointing oil and the fragrant incense; the entryway screen for the entrance to the tabernacle; ¹⁶ the altar of burnt offering with its bronze grate, its poles, and all its utensils; the basin with its stand; ¹⁷ the hangings of the courtyard, its posts and bases, and the screen for the gate of the courtyard; ¹⁸ the tent pegs for the tabernacle and the tent pegs for the courtyard, along with their ropes; ¹⁹ and the specially woven garments for ministering in the sanctuary—the holy garments for the priest Aaron and the garments for his sons to serve as priests."

²⁰ Then the entire Israelite community left Moses's presence. ²¹ Everyone whose heart was moved and whose spirit prompted him came and brought an offering to the Lord for the work on the tent of meeting, for all its services, and for the holy garments. ²² Both men and women came; all who had willing hearts brought brooches, earrings, rings, necklaces, and all kinds of gold jewelry—everyone who presented a presentation offering of gold to the Lord. ²³ Everyone who possessed blue, purple, or scarlet yarn, fine linen or goat hair, ram skins dyed red or fine leather, brought them. ²⁴ Everyone making an offering of silver or bronze brought it as a contribution to the Lord. Everyone who possessed acacia wood useful for any task in the work brought it. ²⁵ Every skilled woman spun yarn with her hands and brought it: blue, purple, and scarlet yarn, and fine linen. ²⁶ And all the women whose hearts were moved spun the goat hair by virtue of their skill. ²⁷ The leaders brought onyx and gemstones to mount on the ephod and breastpiece, ²⁸ as well as the spice and oil for the light, for the anointing oil, and for the fragrant incense. ²⁹ So the Israelites brought a freewill offering to the Lord, all the men and women whose hearts prompted them to bring something for all the work that the Lord, through Moses, had commanded to be done.

BEZALEL AND OHOLIAB

³⁰ Moses then said to the Israelites: "Look, the Lord has appointed by name Bezalel son of Uri, son of Hur, of the tribe of Judah. ³¹ He has filled him with God's Spirit, with wisdom, understanding, and ability in every kind of craft ³² to design artistic works in gold, silver, and bronze, ³³ to cut gemstones for mounting, and to carve wood for work in every kind of artistic craft. ³⁴ He has also

given both him and Oholiab son of Ahisamach, of the tribe of Dan, the ability to teach others. [35] He has filled them with skill to do all the work of a gem cutter; a designer; an embroiderer in blue, purple, and scarlet yarn and fine linen; and a weaver. They can do every kind of craft and design artistic designs."

———

EXODUS 31:3

"I have filled him with God's Spirit, with wisdom, understanding, and ability in every craft..."

———

1 CORINTHIANS 12:4–7, 11 NIV

[4] There are different kinds of gifts, but the same Spirit distributes them. [5] There are different kinds of service, but the same Lord. [6] There are different kinds of working, but in all of them and in everyone it is the same God at work.

[7] Now to each one the manifestation of the Spirit is given for the common good.

…

[11] All these are the work of one and the same Spirit, and he distributes them to each one, just as he determines.

2 PETER 1:3 NLT
GROWING IN FAITH

By his divine power, God has given us everything we need for living a godly life. We have received all of this by coming to know him, the one who called us to himself by means of his marvelous glory and excellence.

1 Summarize the events of
this story.

2 What stood out to you?
What questions do you have?

3 What is God teaching you
in the reading?

Connecting the Stories

All thirty-nine books in the Old Testament combine to tell a single story—the story of God and His love for sinful humanity. This chart shows how the women and men in this study book are connected in God's plan of redemption, which finds ultimate fulfillment in Jesus.

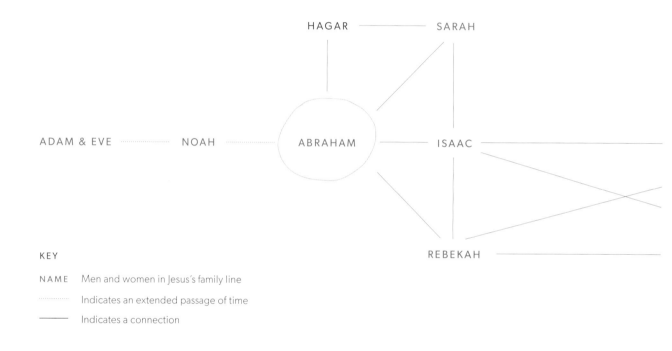

HAGAR ——————— SARAH

ADAM & EVE ·········· NOAH ·········· ABRAHAM ——————— ISAAC

REBEKAH

KEY

NAME   Men and women in Jesus's family line

··········   Indicates an extended passage of time

——————   Indicates a connection

ADAM & EVE: The first people. Created by God in His image.

NOAH: Descended from Adam and Eve's son Seth. God saved Noah and his family from the flood.

ABRAHAM: Descended from Noah's son Shem. God promised to make Abraham into a chosen nation, through whom the entire world would be blessed.

SARAH: Abraham's wife. Gave birth to Isaac, though she was well beyond childbearing age.

HAGAR: Sarah's Egyptian slave who was given to Abraham as a wife; the mother of Ishmael.

ISAAC: Son of Abraham and Sarah, through whom God's promises continued.

REBEKAH: Wife of Isaac; granddaughter of Abraham's brother Nahor; sister of Laban; mother to Esau and Jacob.

ESAU: Eldest son of Isaac and Rebekah; twin brother of Jacob. Did not value his birthright.

JACOB: Youngest son of Isaac and Rebekah; twin brother of Esau. Wrestled with God and received the promises made to his father and grandfather.

LEAH: Daughter of Laban; sister of Rachel; first wife of Jacob; mother of six of Jacob's twelve sons and one daughter.

RACHEL: Daughter of Laban; sister of Leah; second wife of Jacob; mother of Jacob's sons Joseph and Benjamin.

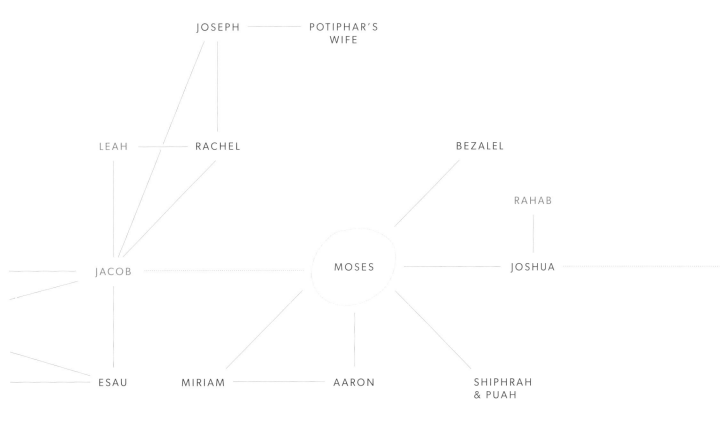

JOSEPH — POTIPHAR'S
WIFE

LEAH — RACHEL

BEZALEL

RAHAB

JACOB   MOSES   JOSHUA

ESAU   MIRIAM — AARON   SHIPHRAH
& PUAH

JOSEPH: Son of Jacob and Rachel. Sold into slavery by his brothers but became a leader in Egypt, a position he used to save the people of the region from a terrible famine.

POTIPHAR'S WIFE: Tried to seduce Joseph, her husband's slave.

SHIPHRAH & PUAH: Egyptian midwives who feared the Lord and refused to kill Hebrew baby boys after the Israelites had multiplied greatly in Egypt.

MOSES: Hebrew slave who was spared as a baby and raised in Pharaoh's household. Called by God to deliver the Israelites out of Egypt. Led God's people for forty years in the wilderness.

AARON: Along with his brother, Moses, was used by God to bring plagues upon Egypt to secure the Israelites' release from Pharaoh. Later became the first high priest of Israel.

MIRIAM: Sister of Moses and Aaron. A prophetess.

BEZALEL: Commissioned by God to be the chief artisan of the tabernacle. Filled with the Holy Spirit to complete his work.

JOSHUA: Moses's assistant who led the Israelites into the promised land after Moses died. Oversaw the initial conquest of Canaan.

RAHAB: A prostitute in Jericho who hid the Israelite spies sent by Joshua. Rewarded with a place among God's people.

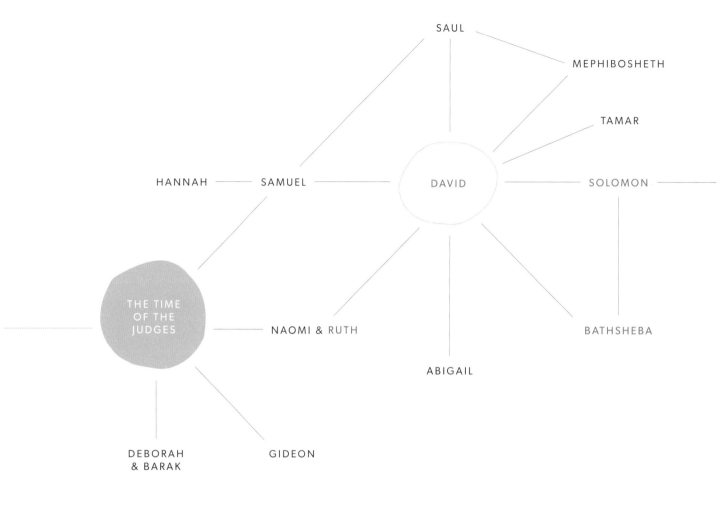

SAUL

MEPHIBOSHETH

TAMAR

HANNAH — SAMUEL — DAVID — SOLOMON

THE TIME
OF THE
JUDGES

NAOMI & RUTH

BATHSHEBA

ABIGAIL

DEBORAH
& BARAK

GIDEON

THE TIME OF THE JUDGES: The generation following Joshua forgot what God had done for them. They entered into repeating cycles of sin, oppression, and deliverance through judges sent by God.

DEBORAH & BARAK: Deborah was a prophetess and judge of Israel; with Barak, she freed the people of Israel from oppression under the Canaanites.

GIDEON: Judge of Israel who defeated the Midianites with an army of three hundred men.

NAOMI & RUTH: Two widows, a mother-in-law and daughter-in-law. God provided Ruth a husband and a legacy from which the kings of Judah came.

HANNAH: Barren woman filled with faith. God opened her womb and gave her children, the first of whom was Samuel.

SAMUEL: Son of Elkanah and Hannah. A prophet and the final judge in Israel who anointed both Saul and David as kings.

SAUL: Anointed by Samuel as the first king of Israel. Ultimately proved to be a man of little faith.

DAVID: A man after God's own heart. Succeeded Saul as king.

ABIGAIL: Widow of Nabal; one of David's wives.

BATHSHEBA: One of David's wives; widow of Uriah the Hittite; mother to Solomon.

TAMAR: Daughter of David; sister of Absalom.

SOLOMON: David and Bathsheba's son. Wise king who compromised in his later years.

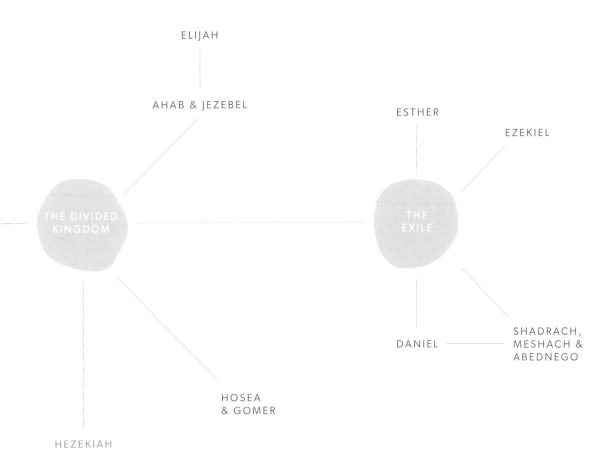

ELIJAH

AHAB & JEZEBEL

ESTHER

EZEKIEL

THE DIVIDED KINGDOM

THE EXILE

SHADRACH, MESHACH & ABEDNEGO

DANIEL

HOSEA & GOMER

HEZEKIAH

THE DIVIDED KINGDOM: After Solomon's death, the nation split in two: the northern kingdom of Israel and the southern kingdom of Judah.

MEPHIBOSHETH: Grandson of Saul; son of David's good friend Jonathan. Welcomed into David's home after the deaths of Saul and Jonathan.

ELIJAH: Prophet of the northern kingdom who predicted a drought. Confronted the prophets of Baal. Prophesied against King Ahab and his wife, Jezebel.

AHAB & JEZEBEL: King and queen of Israel. Did great evil and led the people to worship other gods; confronted by Elijah the prophet.

HOSEA & GOMER: God told the prophet Hosea to marry Gomer, a prostitute, as a living example of Israel's unfaithfulness to the Lord.

HEZEKIAH: King of Judah who removed the centers of idolatry from the land. God answered his prayer to deliver Jerusalem from the hands of the Assyrians.

THE EXILE: In 722 BC, Assyria conquered the northern kingdom and dispersed its people across the empire. In 586 BC, Babylon conquered the south and led its people into captivity.

EZEKIEL: Prophesied during the Babylonian captivity. Wrote against the sins that led to exile and about the faithfulness of God that would bring the people home.

DANIEL: Prophet during the Babylonian captivity. Delivered by God from a den of lions. Foretold the coming of God's kingdom.

SHADRACH, MESHACH & ABEDNEGO: Exiles in Babylon; friends of Daniel. Refused to bow down and worship the golden statue set up by King Nebuchadnezzar.

ESTHER: Jewish exile living in Susa. Chosen to become queen of Persia, putting her in a position to intercede for her people and stop an act of genocide.

Joshua

Strong and Courageous in the Lord

ENCOURAGEMENT OF JOSHUA

¹ After the death of Moses the Lᴏʀᴅ's servant, the Lᴏʀᴅ spoke to Joshua son of Nun, Moses's assistant: ² "Moses my servant is dead. Now you and all the people prepare to cross over the Jordan to the land I am giving the Israelites. ³ I have given you every place where the sole of your foot treads, just as I promised Moses. ⁴ Your territory will be from the wilderness and Lebanon to the great river, the Euphrates River—all the land of the Hittites—and west to the Mediterranean Sea. ⁵ No one will be able to stand against you as long as you live. I will be with you, just as I was with Moses. I will not leave you or abandon you.

⁶ "Be strong and courageous, for you will distribute the land I swore to their fathers to give them as an inheritance. ⁷ Above all, be strong and very courageous to observe carefully the whole instruction my servant Moses commanded you. Do not turn from it to the right or the left, so that you will have success wherever you go. ⁸ This book of instruction must not depart from your mouth; you are to meditate on it day and night so that you may carefully observe everything written in it. For then you will prosper and succeed in whatever you do. ⁹ Haven't I commanded you: be strong and courageous? Do not be afraid or discouraged, for the Lᴏʀᴅ your God is with you wherever you go."

JOSHUA PREPARES THE PEOPLE

¹⁰ Then Joshua commanded the officers of the people: ¹¹ "Go through the camp and tell the people, 'Get provisions ready for yourselves, for within three days you will be crossing the Jordan to go in and take possession of the land the Lᴏʀᴅ your God is giving you to inherit.'"

¹² Joshua said to the Reubenites, the Gadites, and half the tribe of Manasseh: ¹³ "Remember what Moses the Lᴏʀᴅ's servant commanded you when he said, 'The

LORD your God will give you rest, and he will give you this land.' ¹⁴ Your wives, dependents, and livestock may remain in the land Moses gave you on this side of the Jordan. But your best soldiers must cross over in battle formation ahead of your brothers and help them ¹⁵ until the LORD gives your brothers rest, as he has given you, and they too possess the land the LORD your God is giving them. You may then return to the land of your inheritance and take possession of what Moses the LORD's servant gave you on the east side of the Jordan."

¹⁶ They answered Joshua, "Everything you have commanded us we will do, and everywhere you send us we will go. ¹⁷ We will obey you, just as we obeyed Moses in everything. Certainly the LORD your God will be with you, as he was with Moses. ¹⁸ Anyone who rebels against your order and does not obey your words in all that you command him, will be put to death. Above all, be strong and courageous!"

JOSHUA 23
JOSHUA'S FAREWELL ADDRESS

¹ A long time after the LORD had given Israel rest from all the enemies around them, Joshua was old, advanced in age. ² So Joshua summoned all Israel, including its elders, leaders, judges, and officers, and said to them, "I am old, advanced in age, ³ and you have seen for yourselves everything the LORD your God did to all these nations on your account, because it was the LORD your God who was fighting for you. ⁴ See, I have allotted these remaining nations to you as an inheritance for your tribes, including all the nations I have destroyed, from the Jordan westward to the Mediterranean Sea. ⁵ The LORD your God will force them back on your account and drive them out before you so that you can take possession of their land, as the LORD your God promised you.

⁶ "Be very strong and continue obeying all that is written in the book of the law of Moses, so that you do not turn from it to the right or left ⁷ and so that you do not associate with these nations remaining among you. Do not call on the names of their gods or make an oath to them; do not serve them or bow in worship to them. ⁸ Instead, be loyal to the LORD your God, as you have been to this day.

⁹ "The LORD has driven out great and powerful nations before you, and no one is able to stand against you to this day. ¹⁰ One of you routed a thousand because the LORD your God was fighting for you, as he promised. ¹¹ So diligently watch yourselves! Love the LORD your God! ¹² If you ever turn away and become loyal to the rest of these nations remaining among you, and if you intermarry or associate with them and they with you, ¹³ know for certain that the LORD your God will not continue to drive these nations out before you. They will become a snare and a trap for you, a sharp stick for your sides and thorns in your eyes, until you disappear from this good land the LORD your God has given you.

¹⁴ "I am now going the way of the whole earth, and you know with all your heart and all your soul that none of the good promises the Lord your God made to you has failed. Everything was fulfilled for you; not one promise has failed. ¹⁵ Since every good thing the Lord your God promised you has come about, so he will bring on you every bad thing until he has annihilated you from this good land the Lord your God has given you. ¹⁶ If you break the covenant of the Lord your God, which he commanded you, and go and serve other gods, and bow in worship to them, the Lord's anger will burn against you, and you will quickly disappear from this good land he has given you."

———

JOSHUA 1:9

"Do not be afraid or discouraged, for the LORD your God is with you wherever you go."

———

DEUTERONOMY 31:6–8

⁶ Be strong and courageous; don't be terrified or afraid of them. For the Lord your God is the one who will go with you; he will not leave you or abandon you."

⁷ Moses then summoned Joshua and said to him in the sight of all Israel, "Be strong and courageous, for you will go with this people into the land the Lord swore to give to their fathers. You will enable them to take possession of it. ⁸ The Lord is the one who will go before you. He will be with you; he will not leave you or abandon you. Do not be afraid or discouraged."

1   Summarize the events of
    this story.

2   What stood out to you?
    What questions do you have?

3   What is God teaching you
    in the reading?

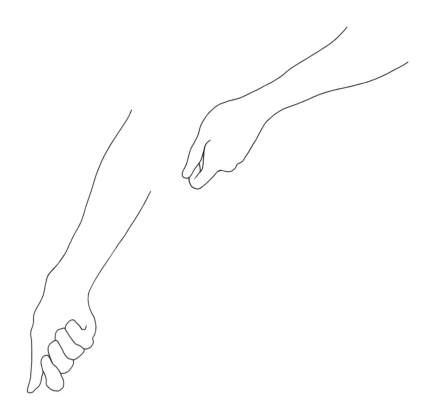

Rahab

The Woman Who Saw What Was Coming

SPIES SENT TO JERICHO

¹ Joshua son of Nun secretly sent two men as spies from the Acacia Grove, saying, "Go and scout the land, especially Jericho." So they left, and they came to the house of a prostitute named Rahab, and stayed there.

² The king of Jericho was told, "Look, some of the Israelite men have come here tonight to investigate the land." ³ Then the king of Jericho sent word to Rahab and said, "Bring out the men who came to you and entered your house, for they came to investigate the entire land."

⁴ But the woman had taken the two men and hidden them. So she said, "Yes, the men did come to me, but I didn't know where they were from. ⁵ At nightfall, when the city gate was about to close, the men went out, and I don't know where they were going. Chase after them quickly, and you can catch up with them!" ⁶ But she had taken them up to the roof and hidden them among the stalks of flax that she had arranged on the roof. ⁷ The men pursued them along the road to the fords of the Jordan, and as soon as they left to pursue them, the city gate was shut.

THE PROMISE TO RAHAB

⁸ Before the men fell asleep, she went up on the roof ⁹ and said to them, "I know that the LORD has given you this land and that the terror of you has fallen on us, and everyone who lives in the land is panicking because of you. ¹⁰ For we have heard how the LORD dried up the water of the Red Sea before you when you came out of Egypt, and what you did to Sihon and Og, the two Amorite kings you completely destroyed across the Jordan. ¹¹ When we heard this, we lost heart, and everyone's courage failed because of you, for the LORD your God is God in heaven above and on earth below. ¹² Now please swear to me by the LORD that you will also show kindness to my father's family, because I showed kindness to you. Give me a sure sign ¹³ that you will spare the lives of my father, mother, brothers, sisters, and all who belong to them, and save us from death."

¹⁴ The men answered her, "We will give our lives for yours. If you don't report our mission, we will show kindness and faithfulness to you when the LORD gives us the land."

¹⁵ Then she let them down by a rope through the window, since she lived in a house that was built into the wall of the city. ¹⁶ "Go to the hill country so that the men pursuing you won't find you," she said to them. "Hide there for three days until they return; afterward, go on your way."

¹⁷ The men said to her, "We will be free from this oath you made us swear, ¹⁸ unless, when we enter the land, you tie this scarlet cord to the window through which you let us down. Bring your father, mother, brothers, and all your father's family into your house. ¹⁹ If anyone goes out the doors of your house, his death will be his own fault, and we will be innocent. But if anyone with you in the house should be harmed, his death will be our fault. ²⁰ And if you report our mission, we are free from the oath you made us swear."

²¹ "Let it be as you say," she replied, and she sent them away. After they had gone, she tied the scarlet cord to the window.

²² So the two men went into the hill country and stayed there three days until the pursuers had returned. They searched all along the way, but did not find them. ²³ Then the men returned, came down from the hill country, and crossed the Jordan. They went to Joshua son of Nun and reported everything that had happened to them. ²⁴ They told Joshua, "The LORD has handed over the entire land to us. Everyone who lives in the land is also panicking because of us."

RAHAB AND HER FAMILY SPARED

²² Joshua said to the two men who had scouted the land, "Go to the prostitute's house and bring the woman out of there, and all who are with her, just as you swore to her." ²³ So the young men who had scouted went in and brought out Rahab and her father, mother, brothers, and all who belonged to her. They brought out her whole family and settled them outside the camp of Israel.

²⁴ They burned the city and everything in it, but they put the silver and gold and the articles of bronze and iron into the treasury of the LORD's house.

Now please swear to me by the LORD that you will also show kindness to my father's family, because I showed kindness to you.

———

²⁵ However, Joshua spared Rahab the prostitute, her father's family, and all who belonged to her, because she hid the messengers Joshua had sent to spy on Jericho, and she still lives in Israel today.

MATTHEW 1:1–6a
THE GENEALOGY OF JESUS CHRIST

¹ An account of the genealogy of Jesus Christ, the Son of David, the Son of Abraham:

FROM ABRAHAM TO DAVID

² Abraham fathered Isaac,
Isaac fathered Jacob,
Jacob fathered Judah and his brothers,
³ Judah fathered Perez and Zerah by Tamar,
Perez fathered Hezron,
Hezron fathered Aram,
⁴ Aram fathered Amminadab,
Amminadab fathered Nahshon,
Nahshon fathered Salmon,
⁵ Salmon fathered Boaz by Rahab,
Boaz fathered Obed by Ruth,
Obed fathered Jesse,
⁶ and Jesse fathered King David.

HEBREWS 11:1, 31
LIVING BY FAITH

¹ Now faith is the reality of what is hoped for, the proof of what is not seen.

…

³¹ By faith Rahab the prostitute welcomed the spies in peace and didn't perish with those who disobeyed.

1   Summarize the events of
    this story.

2   What stood out to you?
    What questions do you have?

3   What is God teaching you
    in the reading?

Peach and Burrata Salad

PREP TIME	SERVINGS
15 minutes	4–6

EMILY MAXSON

@emilysfreshkitchen

INGREDIENTS

5 ounces arugula

8 ounces burrata

3 ounces prosciutto

1–2 peaches

¼ cup pine nuts

¼ cup good quality olive oil

⅛ cup good quality balsamic vinegar

1 teaspoon Dijon mustard

½ teaspoon honey

¼ teaspoon sea salt

INSTRUCTIONS

Place the arugula on a large board or tray.

Cut the burrata into 8 or more pieces and place on top of the arugula.

Arrange pieces of the prosciutto around the burrata.

Slice the peaches and add to the salad.

Sprinkle the pine nuts on top.

Whisk together the olive oil, balsamic vinegar, Dijon, honey, and salt.

Drizzle the dressing over the salad and serve immediately.

Grace Day

Use this day to pray, rest, and reflect on this week's reading,
giving thanks for the grace that is ours in Christ.

By his divine power, God has given us everything we need for living a godly life. We have received all of this by coming to know him, the one who called us to himself by means of his marvelous glory and excellence.

Scripture is God-breathed and true. When we memorize it, we carry the gospel with us wherever we go.

On day 23 we read about Miriam, who sang a song of praise after the Lord provided an escape for the Israelites through the Red Sea. This week we'll memorize Isaiah 12:2, a verse from that day's reading and a reminder that God Himself is our salvation.

Weekly Truth

ISAIAH 12:2

Indeed, God is my salvation;
I will trust him and not be afraid,
for the LORD, the LORD himself,
is my strength and my song.
He has become my salvation.

Find the corresponding memory card in the back of this book.

Deborah and Barak

The Judge and the Reluctant Warrior

JUDGES 4
DEBORAH AND BARAK

[1] The Israelites again did what was evil in the sight of the LORD after Ehud had died. [2] So the LORD sold them to King Jabin of Canaan, who reigned in Hazor. The commander of his army was Sisera who lived in Harosheth of the Nations. [3] Then the Israelites cried out to the LORD, because Jabin had nine hundred iron chariots, and he harshly oppressed them twenty years.

[4] Deborah, a prophetess and the wife of Lappidoth, was judging Israel at that time. [5] She would sit under the palm tree of Deborah between Ramah and Bethel in the hill country of Ephraim, and the Israelites went up to her to settle disputes.

[6] She summoned Barak son of Abinoam from Kedesh in Naphtali and said to him, "Hasn't the LORD, the God of Israel, commanded you: 'Go, deploy the troops on Mount Tabor, and take with you ten thousand men from the Naphtalites and Zebulunites? [7] Then I will lure Sisera commander of Jabin's army, his chariots, and his infantry at the Wadi Kishon to fight against you, and I will hand him over to you.'"

[8] Barak said to her, "If you will go with me, I will go. But if you will not go with me, I will not go."

[9] "I will gladly go with you," she said, "but you will receive no honor on the road you are about to take, because the LORD will sell Sisera to a woman." So Deborah got up and went with Barak to Kedesh. [10] Barak summoned Zebulun and Naphtali to Kedesh; ten thousand men followed him, and Deborah also went with him.

[11] Now Heber the Kenite had moved away from the Kenites, the sons of Hobab, Moses's father-in-law, and pitched his tent beside the oak tree of Zaanannim, which was near Kedesh.

[12] It was reported to Sisera that Barak son of Abinoam had gone up Mount Tabor. [13] Sisera summoned all his nine hundred iron chariots and all the troops who were with him from Harosheth of the Nations to the Wadi Kishon. [14] Then Deborah said to Barak, "Go! This is the day the LORD has handed Sisera over to you. Hasn't the LORD gone before you?" So Barak came down from Mount Tabor with ten thousand men following him.

[15] The LORD threw Sisera, all his charioteers, and all his army into a panic before Barak's assault. Sisera left his chariot and fled on foot. [16] Barak pursued the chariots and the army as far as Harosheth of the Nations, and the whole army of Sisera fell by the sword; not a single man was left.

17 Meanwhile, Sisera had fled on foot to the tent of Jael, the wife of Heber the Kenite, because there was peace between King Jabin of Hazor and the family of Heber the Kenite. 18 Jael went out to greet Sisera and said to him, "Come in, my lord. Come in with me. Don't be afraid." So he went into her tent, and she covered him with a blanket. 19 He said to her, "Please give me a little water to drink for I am thirsty." She opened a container of milk, gave him a drink, and covered him again. 20 Then he said to her, "Stand at the entrance to the tent. If a man comes and asks you, 'Is there a man here?' say, 'No.'" 21 While he was sleeping from exhaustion, Heber's wife Jael took a tent peg, grabbed a hammer, and went silently to Sisera. She hammered the peg into his temple and drove it into the ground, and he died.

22 When Barak arrived in pursuit of Sisera, Jael went out to greet him and said to him, "Come and I will show you the man you are looking for." So he went in with her, and there was Sisera lying dead with a tent peg through his temple!

23 That day God subdued King Jabin of Canaan before the Israelites. 24 The power of the Israelites continued to increase against King Jabin of Canaan until they destroyed him.

JUDGES 5
DEBORAH'S SONG

1 On that day Deborah and Barak son of Abinoam sang:

2 When the leaders lead in Israel,
when the people volunteer,
blessed be the LORD.
3 Listen, kings! Pay attention, princes!
I will sing to the LORD;
I will sing praise to the LORD God of Israel.
4 LORD, when you came from Seir,
when you marched from the fields of Edom,
the earth trembled,
the skies poured rain,
and the clouds poured water.
5 The mountains melted before the LORD,
even Sinai, before the LORD, the God of Israel.

6 In the days of Shamgar son of Anath,
in the days of Jael,
the main roads were deserted
because travelers kept to the side roads.
7 Villages were deserted,
they were deserted in Israel,
until I, Deborah, arose,
a mother in Israel.
8 Israel chose new gods,
then there was war in the city gates.
Not a shield or spear was seen
among forty thousand in Israel.
9 My heart is with the leaders of Israel,
with the volunteers of the people.
Blessed be the LORD!
10 You who ride on white donkeys,
who sit on saddle blankets,
and who travel on the road, give praise!
11 Let them tell the righteous acts of the LORD,
the righteous deeds of his warriors in Israel,
with the voices of the singers at the watering places.
Then the LORD's people went down to the city gates.
12 "Awake! Awake, Deborah!
Awake! Awake, sing a song!
Arise, Barak,
and take your prisoners,
son of Abinoam!"
13 Then the survivors came down to the nobles;
the LORD's people came down to me with the warriors.
14 Those with their roots in Amalek came
from Ephraim;
Benjamin came with your people after you.
The leaders came down from Machir,
and those who carry a marshal's staff came from Zebulun.
15 The princes of Issachar were with Deborah;
Issachar was with Barak;
they were under his leadership in the valley.
There was great searching of heart
among the clans of Reuben.
16 Why did you sit among the sheep pens
listening to the playing of pipes for the flocks?
There was great searching of heart
among the clans of Reuben.

¹⁷ Gilead remained beyond the Jordan.
Dan, why did you linger at the ships?
Asher remained at the seashore
and stayed in his harbors.
¹⁸ The people of Zebulun defied death,
Naphtali also, on the heights of the battlefield.

¹⁹ Kings came and fought.
Then the kings of Canaan fought
at Taanach by the Waters of Megiddo,
but they did not plunder the silver.
²⁰ The stars fought from the heavens;
the stars fought with Sisera from their paths.
²¹ The river Kishon swept them away,
the ancient river, the river Kishon.
March on, my soul, in strength!
²² The horses' hooves then hammered—
the galloping, galloping of his stallions.
²³ "Curse Meroz," says the angel of the LORD,
"Bitterly curse her inhabitants,
for they did not come to help the LORD,
to help the LORD with the warriors."

²⁴ Jael is most blessed of women,
the wife of Heber the Kenite;
she is most blessed among tent-dwelling women.
²⁵ He asked for water; she gave him milk.
She brought him cream in a majestic bowl.
²⁶ She reached for a tent peg,
her right hand, for a workman's hammer.
Then she hammered Sisera—
she crushed his head;
she shattered and pierced his temple.
²⁷ He collapsed, he fell, he lay down between her feet;
he collapsed, he fell between her feet;
where he collapsed, there he fell—dead.

²⁸ Sisera's mother looked through the window;
she peered through the lattice, crying out:
"Why is his chariot so long in coming?
Why don't I hear the hoofbeats of his horses?"

²⁹ Her wisest princesses answer her;
she even answers herself:
³⁰ "Are they not finding and dividing the spoil—
a girl or two for each warrior,
the spoil of colored garments for Sisera,
the spoil of an embroidered garment or two for my neck?"

³¹ LORD, may all your enemies perish as Sisera did.
But may those who love him
be like the rising of the sun in its strength.

And the land had peace for forty years.

DEUTERONOMY 20:1–4

¹ When you go out to war against your enemies and see horses, chariots, and an army larger than yours, do not be afraid of them, for the LORD your God, who brought you out of the land of Egypt, is with you. ² When you are about to engage in battle, the priest is to come forward and address the army. ³ He is to say to them: "Listen, Israel: Today you are about to engage in battle with your enemies. Do not be cowardly. Do not be afraid, alarmed, or terrified because of them. ⁴ For the LORD your God is the one who goes with you to fight for you against your enemies to give you victory."

1 Summarize the events of
   this story.

2 What stood out to you?
   What questions do you have?

3 What is God teaching you
   in the reading?

Gideon

The Judge Who Asked for a Sign

[11] The angel of the LORD came, and he sat under the oak that was in Ophrah, which belonged to Joash, the Abiezrite. His son Gideon was threshing wheat in the winepress in order to hide it from the Midianites. [12] Then the angel of the LORD appeared to him and said: "The LORD is with you, valiant warrior."

[13] Gideon said to him, "Please, my lord, if the LORD is with us, why has all this happened? And where are all his wonders that our fathers told us about? They said, 'Hasn't the LORD brought us out of Egypt?' But now the LORD has abandoned us and handed us over to Midian."

[14] The LORD turned to him and said, "Go in the strength you have and deliver Israel from the grasp of Midian. I am sending you!"

[15] He said to him, "Please, Lord, how can I deliver Israel? Look, my family is the weakest in Manasseh, and I am the youngest in my father's family."

[16] "But I will be with you," the LORD said to him. "You will strike Midian down as if it were one man."

[17] Then he said to him, "If I have found favor with you, give me a sign that you are speaking with me. [18] Please do not leave this place until I return to you. Let me bring my gift and set it before you."

And he said, "I will stay until you return."

[19] So Gideon went and prepared a young goat and unleavened bread from a half bushel of flour. He placed the meat in a basket and the broth in a pot. He brought them out and offered them to him under the oak.

20 The angel of God said to him, "Take the meat with the unleavened bread, put it on this stone, and pour the broth on it." So he did that.

21 The angel of the LORD extended the tip of the staff that was in his hand and touched the meat and the unleavened bread. Fire came up from the rock and consumed the meat and the unleavened bread. Then the angel of the LORD vanished from his sight.

22 When Gideon realized that he was the angel of the LORD, he said, "Oh no, Lord GOD! I have seen the angel of the LORD face to face!"

23 But the LORD said to him, "Peace to you. Don't be afraid, for you will not die."

…

THE SIGN OF THE FLEECE

33 All the Midianites, Amalekites, and Qedemites gathered together, crossed over the Jordan, and camped in the Jezreel Valley.

34 The Spirit of the LORD enveloped Gideon, and he blew the ram's horn and the Abiezrites rallied behind him. 35 He sent messengers throughout all of Manasseh, who rallied behind him. He also sent messengers throughout Asher, Zebulun, and Naphtali, who also came to meet him.

36 Then Gideon said to God, "If you will deliver Israel by my hand, as you said, 37 I will put a wool fleece here on the threshing floor. If dew is only on the fleece, and all the ground is dry, I will know that you will deliver Israel by my strength, as you said." 38 And that is what happened. When he got up early in the morning, he squeezed the fleece and wrung dew out of it, filling a bowl with water.

39 Gideon then said to God, "Don't be angry with me; let me speak one more time. Please allow me to make one more test with the fleece. Let it remain dry, and the dew be all over the ground." 40 That night God did as Gideon requested: only the fleece was dry, and dew was all over the ground.

JUDGES 7:1–23
GOD SELECTS GIDEON'S ARMY

1 Jerubbaal (that is, Gideon) and all the troops who were with him, got up early and camped beside the spring of Harod. The camp of Midian was north of them, below the hill of Moreh, in the valley. 2 The LORD said to Gideon, "You have too many troops for me to hand the Midianites over to them, or else Israel might elevate themselves over me and say, 'My own strength saved me.' 3 Now announce to the troops: 'Whoever is fearful and trembling may turn back and leave Mount Gilead.'" So twenty-two thousand of the troops turned back, but ten thousand remained.

4 Then the LORD said to Gideon, "There are still too many troops. Take them down to the water, and I will test them for you there. If I say to you, 'This one can go with you,' he can go. But if I say about anyone, 'This one cannot go with you,' he cannot go." 5 So he brought the troops down to the water, and the LORD said to Gideon, "Separate everyone who laps water with his tongue like a dog. Do the same with everyone who kneels to drink." 6 The number of those who lapped with their hands to their mouths was three hundred men, and all the rest of the troops knelt to drink water. 7 The LORD said to Gideon, "I will deliver you with the three hundred men who lapped and hand the Midianites over to you. But everyone else is to go home." 8 So Gideon sent all the Israelites to their tents but kept the three hundred troops, who took the provisions and their trumpets. The camp of Midian was below him in the valley.

GIDEON SPIES ON THE MIDIANITE CAMP

9 That night the LORD said to him, "Get up and attack the camp, for I have handed it over to you. 10 But if you are afraid to attack the camp, go down with Purah your servant. 11 Listen to what they say, and then you will be encouraged to attack the camp." So he went down with Purah his servant to the outpost of the troops who were in the camp.

12 Now the Midianites, Amalekites, and all the Qedemites had settled down in the valley like a swarm of locusts, and their camels were as innumerable as the sand on the seashore. 13 When Gideon arrived, there was a man telling his friend about a dream. He said, "Listen, I had a dream: a loaf of

Then the angel of the LORD appeared to him and said: "The LORD is with you, valiant warrior."

———

barley bread came tumbling into the Midianite camp, struck a tent, and it fell. The loaf turned the tent upside down so that it collapsed."

14 His friend answered: "This is nothing less than the sword of Gideon son of Joash, the Israelite. God has handed the entire Midianite camp over to him."

GIDEON ATTACKS THE MIDIANITES

15 When Gideon heard the account of the dream and its interpretation, he bowed in worship. He returned to Israel's camp and said, "Get up, for the LORD has handed the Midianite camp over to you." 16 Then he divided the three hundred men into three companies and gave each of the men a trumpet in one hand and an empty pitcher with a torch inside it in the other hand.

17 "Watch me," he said to them, "and do what I do. When I come to the outpost of the camp, do as I do. 18 When I and everyone with me blow our trumpets, you are also to blow your trumpets all around the camp. Then you will say, 'For the LORD and for Gideon!'"

19 Gideon and the hundred men who were with him went to the outpost of the camp at the beginning of the middle watch after the sentries had been stationed. They blew their trumpets and broke the pitchers that were in their hands. 20 The three companies blew their trumpets and shattered their pitchers. They held their torches in their left hands, their trumpets in their right hands, and shouted, "A sword for the LORD and for Gideon!" 21 Each Israelite took his

position around the camp, and the entire Midianite army began to run, and they cried out as they fled. 22 When Gideon's men blew their three hundred trumpets, the LORD caused the men in the whole army to turn on each other with their swords. They fled to Acacia House in the direction of Zererah as far as the border of Abel-meholah near Tabbath. 23 Then the men of Israel were called from Naphtali, Asher, and Manasseh, and they pursued the Midianites.

PSALM 9:3–10

3 When my enemies retreat,
they stumble and perish before you.
4 For you have upheld my just cause;
you are seated on your throne as a righteous judge.
5 You have rebuked the nations:
You have destroyed the wicked;
you have erased their name forever and ever.
6 The enemy has come to eternal ruin.
You have uprooted the cities,
and the very memory of them has perished.

7 But the LORD sits enthroned forever;
he has established his throne for judgment.
8 And he judges the world with righteousness;
he executes judgment on the nations with fairness.
9 The LORD is a refuge for the persecuted,
a refuge in times of trouble.
10 Those who know your name trust in you
because you have not abandoned
those who seek you, LORD.

1   Summarize the events of
     this story.

2   What stood out to you?
     What questions do you have?

3   What is God teaching you
     in the reading?

Naomi and Ruth

A Family Redeemed and Restored

NAOMI'S FAMILY IN MOAB

1 During the time of the judges, there was a famine in the land. A man left Bethlehem in Judah with his wife and two sons to stay in the territory of Moab for a while. 2 The man's name was Elimelech, and his wife's name was Naomi. The names of his two sons were Mahlon and Chilion. They were Ephrathites from Bethlehem in Judah. They entered the fields of Moab and settled there. 3 Naomi's husband Elimelech died, and she was left with her two sons. 4 Her sons took Moabite women as their wives: one was named Orpah and the second was named Ruth. After they lived in Moab about ten years, 5 both Mahlon and Chilion also died, and Naomi was left without her two children and without her husband.

RUTH'S LOYALTY TO NAOMI

6 She and her daughters-in-law set out to return from the territory of Moab, because she had heard in Moab that the LORD had paid attention to his people's need by providing them food. 7 She left the place where she had been living, accompanied by her two daughters-in-law, and traveled along the road leading back to the land of Judah.

8 Naomi said to them, "Each of you go back to your mother's home. May the LORD show kindness to you as you have shown to the dead and to me. 9 May the LORD grant each of you rest in the house of a new husband." She kissed them, and they wept loudly.

10 They said to her, "We insist on returning with you to your people."

11 But Naomi replied, "Return home, my daughters. Why do you want to go with me? Am I able to have any more sons who could become your husbands? 12 Return home, my daughters. Go on, for I am too old to have another husband. Even if I thought there was still hope for me to have a husband tonight and to bear sons, 13 would you be willing to wait for them to grow up? Would you restrain yourselves from remarrying? No, my daughters, my life is much too bitter for you to share, because the LORD's hand has turned against me." 14 Again they wept loudly, and Orpah kissed her mother-in-law, but Ruth clung to her. 15 Naomi said, "Look, your sister-in-law has gone back to her people and to her gods. Follow your sister-in-law."

16 But Ruth replied:

> Don't plead with me to abandon you
> or to return and not follow you.
> For wherever you go, I will go,
> and wherever you live, I will live;
> your people will be my people,
> and your God will be my God.

The women said to Naomi, "Blessed be the LORD, who has not left you without a family redeemer today. May his name become well known in Israel."

———

17 Where you die, I will die,
and there I will be buried.
May the LORD punish me,
and do so severely,
if anything but death separates you and me.

18 When Naomi saw that Ruth was determined to go with her, she stopped talking to her.

19 The two of them traveled until they came to Bethlehem. When they entered Bethlehem, the whole town was excited about their arrival and the local women exclaimed, "Can this be Naomi?"

20 "Don't call me Naomi. Call me Mara," she answered, "for the Almighty has made me very bitter. 21 I went away full, but the LORD has brought me back empty. Why do you call me Naomi, since the LORD has opposed me, and the Almighty has afflicted me?"

RUTH 2:1–13, 18–20
RUTH AND BOAZ MEET

1 Now Naomi had a relative on her husband's side. He was a prominent man of noble character from Elimelech's family. His name was Boaz.

2 Ruth the Moabitess asked Naomi, "Will you let me go into the fields and gather fallen grain behind someone with whom I find favor?"

Naomi answered her, "Go ahead, my daughter." 3 So Ruth left and entered the field to gather grain behind the harvesters. She happened to be in the portion of the field belonging to Boaz, who was from Elimelech's family.

4 Later, when Boaz arrived from Bethlehem, he said to the harvesters, "The LORD be with you."

"The LORD bless you," they replied.

5 Boaz asked his servant who was in charge of the harvesters, "Whose young woman is this?"

6 The servant answered, "She is the young Moabite woman who returned with Naomi from the territory of Moab. 7 She asked, 'Will you let me gather fallen grain among the bundles behind the harvesters?' She came and has been on her feet since early morning, except that she rested a little in the shelter."

8 Then Boaz said to Ruth, "Listen, my daughter. Don't go and gather grain in another field, and don't leave this one,

but stay here close to my female servants. ⁹ See which field they are harvesting, and follow them. Haven't I ordered the young men not to touch you? When you are thirsty, go and drink from the jars the young men have filled."

¹⁰ She fell facedown, bowed to the ground, and said to him, "Why have I found favor with you, so that you notice me, although I am a foreigner?"

¹¹ Boaz answered her, "Everything you have done for your mother-in-law since your husband's death has been fully reported to me: how you left your father and mother and your native land, and how you came to a people you didn't previously know. ¹² May the LORD reward you for what you have done, and may you receive a full reward from the LORD God of Israel, under whose wings you have come for refuge."

¹³ "My lord," she said, "I have found favor with you, for you have comforted and encouraged your servant, although I am not like one of your female servants."

…

¹⁸ She picked up the grain and went into the town, where her mother-in-law saw what she had gleaned. She brought out what she had left over from her meal and gave it to her.

¹⁹ Her mother-in-law said to her, "Where did you gather barley today, and where did you work? May the LORD bless the man who noticed you."

Ruth told her mother-in-law whom she had worked with and said, "The name of the man I worked with today is Boaz."

²⁰ Then Naomi said to her daughter-in-law, "May the LORD bless him because he has not abandoned his kindness to the living or the dead." Naomi continued, "The man is a close relative. He is one of our family redeemers."

RUTH 3:1–11
RUTH'S APPEAL TO BOAZ

¹ Ruth's mother-in-law Naomi said to her, "My daughter, shouldn't I find rest for you, so that you will be taken care of? ² Now isn't Boaz our relative? Haven't you been working with his female servants? This evening he will be winnowing barley on the threshing floor. ³ Wash, put on perfumed oil, and wear your best clothes. Go down to the threshing floor, but don't let the man know you are there until he has finished eating and drinking. ⁴ When he lies down, notice the place where he's lying, go in and uncover his feet, and lie down. Then he will explain to you what you should do."

⁵ So Ruth said to her, "I will do everything you say." ⁶ She went down to the threshing floor and did everything her mother-in-law had charged her to do. ⁷ After Boaz ate, drank, and was in good spirits, he went to lie down at the end of the pile of barley, and she came secretly, uncovered his feet, and lay down.

⁸ At midnight, Boaz was startled, turned over, and there lying at his feet was a woman! ⁹ So he asked, "Who are you?"

"I am Ruth, your servant," she replied. "Take me under your wing, for you are a family redeemer."

¹⁰ Then he said, "May the LORD bless you, my daughter. You have shown more kindness now than before, because you have not pursued younger men, whether rich or poor. ¹¹ Now don't be afraid, my daughter. I will do for you whatever you say, since all the people in my town know that you are a woman of noble character."

RUTH 4:13–17

¹³ Boaz took Ruth and she became his wife. He slept with her, and the LORD granted conception to her, and she gave birth to a son. ¹⁴ The women said to Naomi, "Blessed be the LORD, who has not left you without a family redeemer today. May his name become well known in Israel. ¹⁵ He will renew your life and sustain you in your old age. Indeed, your daughter-in-law, who loves you and is better to you than seven sons, has given birth to him." ¹⁶ Naomi took the child, placed him on her lap, and became his nanny. ¹⁷ The neighbor women said, "A son has been born to Naomi," and they named him Obed. He was the father of Jesse, the father of David.

PROVERBS 31:10–31
IN PRAISE OF A WIFE OF NOBLE CHARACTER

¹⁰ Who can find a wife of noble character?
She is far more precious than jewels.
¹¹ The heart of her husband trusts in her,
and he will not lack anything good.

¹² She rewards him with good, not evil,
all the days of her life.
¹³ She selects wool and flax
and works with willing hands.
¹⁴ She is like the merchant ships,
bringing her food from far away.
¹⁵ She rises while it is still night
and provides food for her household
and portions for her female servants.
¹⁶ She evaluates a field and buys it;
she plants a vineyard with her earnings.
¹⁷ She draws on her strength
and reveals that her arms are strong.
¹⁸ She sees that her profits are good,
and her lamp never goes out at night.
¹⁹ She extends her hands to the spinning staff,
and her hands hold the spindle.
²⁰ Her hands reach out to the poor,
and she extends her hands to the needy.
²¹ She is not afraid for her household when it snows,
for all in her household are doubly clothed.
²² She makes her own bed coverings;
her clothing is fine linen and purple.
²³ Her husband is known at the city gates,
where he sits among the elders of the land.
²⁴ She makes and sells linen garments;
she delivers belts to the merchants.
²⁵ Strength and honor are her clothing,
and she can laugh at the time to come.
²⁶ Her mouth speaks wisdom,
and loving instruction is on her tongue.
²⁷ She watches over the activities of her household
and is never idle.
²⁸ Her children rise up and call her blessed;
her husband also praises her:
²⁹ "Many women have done noble deeds,
but you surpass them all!"
³⁰ Charm is deceptive and beauty is fleeting,
but a woman who fears the LORD will be praised.
³¹ Give her the reward of her labor,
and let her works praise her at the city gates.

1 Summarize the events of
this story.

2 What stood out to you?
What questions do you have?

3 What is God teaching you
in the reading?

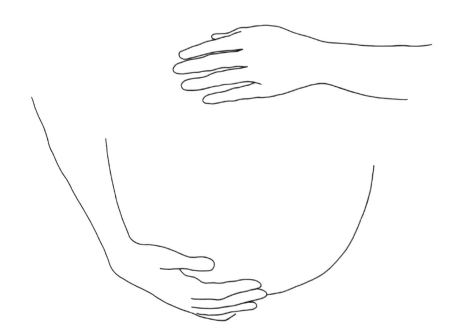

Hannah

The Childless Wife Heard by God

HANNAH'S VOW

¹ There was a man from Ramathaim-zophim in the hill country of Ephraim. His name was Elkanah son of Jeroham, son of Elihu, son of Tohu, son of Zuph, an Ephraimite. ² He had two wives, the first named Hannah and the second Peninnah. Peninnah had children, but Hannah was childless. ³ This man would go up from his town every year to worship and to sacrifice to the LORD of Armies at Shiloh, where Eli's two sons, Hophni and Phinehas, were the LORD's priests.

⁴ Whenever Elkanah offered a sacrifice, he always gave portions of the meat to his wife Peninnah and to each of her sons and daughters. ⁵ But he gave a double portion to Hannah, for he loved her even though the LORD had kept her from conceiving. ⁶ Her rival would taunt her severely just to provoke her, because the LORD had kept Hannah from conceiving. ⁷ Year after year, when she went up to the LORD's house, her rival taunted her in this way. Hannah would weep and would not eat. ⁸ "Hannah, why are you crying?" her husband Elkanah would ask. "Why won't you eat? Why are you troubled? Am I not better to you than ten sons?"

⁹ On one occasion, Hannah got up after they ate and drank at Shiloh. The priest Eli was sitting on a chair by the doorpost of the LORD's temple. ¹⁰ Deeply hurt, Hannah prayed to the LORD and wept with many tears. ¹¹ Making a vow, she pleaded, "LORD of Armies, if you will take notice of your servant's affliction, remember and not forget me, and give your servant a son, I will give him to the LORD all the days of his life, and his hair will never be cut."

¹² While she continued praying in the LORD's presence, Eli watched her mouth. ¹³ Hannah was praying silently, and though her lips were moving, her voice could not be heard. Eli thought she was drunk ¹⁴ and said to her, "How long are you going to be drunk? Get rid of your wine!"

¹⁵ "No, my lord," Hannah replied. "I am a woman with a broken heart. I haven't had any wine or beer; I've been pouring out my heart before the LORD. ¹⁶ Don't think of me as a wicked woman; I've been praying from the depth of my anguish and resentment."

¹⁷ Eli responded, "Go in peace, and may the God of Israel grant the request you've made of him."

¹⁸ "May your servant find favor with you," she replied. Then Hannah went on her way; she ate and no longer looked despondent.

SAMUEL'S BIRTH AND DEDICATION

¹⁹ The next morning Elkanah and Hannah got up early to worship before the LORD. Afterward, they returned home to Ramah. Then Elkanah was intimate with his wife Hannah, and the LORD remembered her. ²⁰ After some time, Hannah conceived and gave birth to a son. She named him Samuel, because she said, "I requested him from the LORD."

²¹ When Elkanah and all his household went up to make the annual sacrifice and his vow offering to the LORD, ²² Hannah did not go and explained to her husband, "After the child is weaned, I'll take him to appear in the LORD's presence and to stay there permanently."

²³ Her husband Elkanah replied, "Do what you think is best, and stay here until you've weaned him. May the LORD confirm your word." So Hannah stayed there and nursed her son until she weaned him. ²⁴ When she had weaned him, she took him with her to Shiloh, as well as a three-year-old bull, half a bushel of flour, and a clay jar of wine. Though the boy was still young, she took him to the LORD's house at Shiloh. ²⁵ Then they slaughtered the bull and brought the boy to Eli.

²⁶ "Please, my lord," she said, "as surely as you live, my lord, I am the woman who stood here beside you praying to the LORD. ²⁷ I prayed for this boy, and since the LORD gave me what I asked him for, ²⁸ I now give the boy to the LORD. For as long as he lives, he is given to the LORD." Then he worshiped the LORD there.

There is no one holy like the LORD.
There is no one besides you!
And there is no rock like our God.

---

1 SAMUEL 2:1–11
HANNAH'S TRIUMPHANT PRAYER

¹ Hannah prayed:

My heart rejoices in the LORD;
my horn is lifted up by the LORD.
My mouth boasts over my enemies,
because I rejoice in your salvation.
² There is no one holy like the LORD.
There is no one besides you!
And there is no rock like our God.
³ Do not boast so proudly,
or let arrogant words come out of your mouth,
for the LORD is a God of knowledge,
and actions are weighed by him.
⁴ The bows of the warriors are broken,
but the feeble are clothed with strength.
⁵ Those who are full hire themselves out for food,
but those who are starving hunger no more.
The woman who is childless gives birth to seven,
but the woman with many sons pines away.
⁶ The LORD brings death and gives life;
he sends some down to Sheol, and he raises others up.
⁷ The LORD brings poverty and gives wealth;
he humbles and he exalts.
⁸ He raises the poor from the dust
and lifts the needy from the trash heap.
He seats them with noblemen
and gives them a throne of honor.

For the foundations of the earth are the LORD's;
he has set the world on them.
⁹ He guards the steps of his faithful ones,
but the wicked perish in darkness,
for a person does not prevail by his own strength.
¹⁰ Those who oppose the LORD will be shattered;
he will thunder in the heavens against them.
The LORD will judge the ends of the earth.
He will give power to his king;
he will lift up the horn of his anointed.

¹¹ Elkanah went home to Ramah, but the boy served the LORD in the presence of the priest Eli.

PHILIPPIANS 4:4–7

⁴ Rejoice in the Lord always. I will say it again: Rejoice! ⁵ Let your graciousness be known to everyone. The Lord is near. ⁶ Don't worry about anything, but in everything, through prayer and petition with thanksgiving, present your requests to God. ⁷ And the peace of God, which surpasses all understanding, will guard your hearts and minds in Christ Jesus.

1 Summarize the events of
   this story.

2 What stood out to you?
   What questions do you have?

3 What is God teaching you
   in the reading?

Samuel

A Mouthpiece of the Lord

1 SAMUEL 2:12–26
ELI'S FAMILY JUDGED

¹² Eli's sons were wicked men; they did not respect the LORD ¹³ or the priests' share of the sacrifices from the people. When anyone offered a sacrifice, the priest's servant would come with a three-pronged meat fork while the meat was boiling ¹⁴ and plunge it into the container, kettle, cauldron, or cooking pot. The priest would claim for himself whatever the meat fork brought up. This is the way they treated all the Israelites who came there to Shiloh. ¹⁵ Even before the fat was burned, the priest's servant would come and say to the one who was sacrificing, "Give the priest some meat to roast, because he won't accept boiled meat from you—only raw." ¹⁶ If that person said to him, "The fat must be burned first; then you can take whatever you want for yourself," the servant would reply, "No, I insist that you hand it over right now. If you don't, I'll take it by force!" ¹⁷ So the servants' sin was very severe in the presence of the LORD, because the men treated the LORD's offering with contempt.

¹⁸ Samuel served in the LORD's presence—this mere boy was dressed in the linen ephod. ¹⁹ Each year his mother made him a little robe and took it to him when she went with her husband to offer the annual sacrifice. ²⁰ Eli would bless Elkanah and his wife: "May the LORD give you children by this woman in place of the one she has given to the LORD." Then they would go home.

²¹ The LORD paid attention to Hannah's need, and she conceived and gave birth to three sons and two daughters. Meanwhile, the boy Samuel grew up in the presence of the LORD.

²² Now Eli was very old. He heard about everything his sons were doing to all Israel and how they were sleeping with the women who served at the entrance to the tent of meeting. ²³ He said to them, "Why are you doing these things? I have heard about your evil actions from all these people. ²⁴ No, my sons, the news I hear the LORD's people spreading is not good. ²⁵ If one person sins against another, God can intercede for him, but if a person sins against the LORD, who can intercede for him?" But they would not listen to their father, since the LORD intended to kill them. ²⁶ By contrast, the boy Samuel grew in stature and in favor with the LORD and with people.

1 SAMUEL 3
SAMUEL'S CALL

¹ The boy Samuel served the LORD in Eli's presence. In those days the word of the LORD was rare and prophetic visions were not widespread.

² One day Eli, whose eyesight was failing, was lying in his usual place. ³ Before the lamp of God had gone out, Samuel was lying down in the temple of the Lord, where the ark of God was located.

⁴ Then the Lord called Samuel, and he answered, "Here I am." ⁵ He ran to Eli and said, "Here I am; you called me."

"I didn't call," Eli replied. "Go back and lie down." So he went and lay down.

⁶ Once again the Lord called, "Samuel!"

Samuel got up, went to Eli, and said, "Here I am; you called me."

"I didn't call, my son," he replied. "Go back and lie down."

⁷ Now Samuel did not yet know the Lord, because the word of the Lord had not yet been revealed to him. ⁸ Once again, for the third time, the Lord called Samuel. He got up, went to Eli, and said, "Here I am; you called me."

Then Eli understood that the Lord was calling the boy. ⁹ He told Samuel, "Go and lie down. If he calls you, say, 'Speak, Lord, for your servant is listening.'" So Samuel went and lay down in his place.

¹⁰ The Lord came, stood there, and called as before, "Samuel, Samuel!"

Samuel responded, "Speak, for your servant is listening."

¹¹ The Lord said to Samuel, "I am about to do something in Israel that everyone who hears about it will shudder. ¹² On that day I will carry out against Eli everything I said about his family, from beginning to end. ¹³ I told him that I am going to judge his family forever because of the iniquity he knows about: his sons are cursing God, and he has not stopped them. ¹⁴ Therefore, I have sworn to Eli's family: The iniquity of Eli's family will never be wiped out by either sacrifice or offering."

¹⁵ Samuel lay down until the morning; then he opened the doors of the Lord's house. He was afraid to tell Eli the vision, ¹⁶ but Eli called him and said, "Samuel, my son."

"Here I am," answered Samuel.

¹⁷ "What was the message he gave you?" Eli asked. "Don't hide it from me. May God punish you and do so severely if you hide anything from me that he told you." ¹⁸ So Samuel told him everything and did not hide anything from him. Eli responded, "He is the Lord. Let him do what he thinks is good."

¹⁹ Samuel grew, and the Lord was with him, and he fulfilled everything Samuel prophesied. ²⁰ All Israel from Dan to Beer-sheba knew that Samuel was a confirmed prophet of the Lord. ²¹ The Lord continued to appear in Shiloh, because there he revealed himself to Samuel by his word.

EXODUS 27:20–21
THE LAMPSTAND OIL

²⁰ "You are to command the Israelites to bring you pure oil from crushed olives for the light, in order to keep the lamp burning regularly. ²¹ In the tent of meeting outside the curtain that is in front of the testimony, Aaron and his sons are to tend the lamp from evening until morning before the Lord. This is to be a permanent statute for the Israelites throughout their generations."

1   Summarize the events of
this story.

2   What stood out to you?
What questions do you have?

3   What is God teaching you
in the reading?

Creamy Lemon Bars

PREP TIME	BAKE TIME	SERVINGS
15 minutes	40 minutes	12–16

INGREDIENTS

CRUST

1 box yellow cake mix

8 tablespoons unsalted butter, melted

1 egg

FILLING

3 cups sweetened condensed milk

3 eggs yolks, room temperature

⅔ cup freshly squeezed lemon juice, about 3–4 lemons

¼ teaspoon coarse kosher salt

Powdered sugar, for garnish

INSTRUCTIONS

Preheat oven to 350°F.

Place cake mix and melted butter in the bowl of an electric mixer fitted with the paddle attachment. Mix on medium speed until just combined.

Add egg with the mixer on low for 1 to 2 minutes.

Lightly pat dough evenly on the bottom of a 9x13-inch pan lined with parchment paper, leaving an overhang on two sides. The parchment paper will allow you to lift the bars out of the pan easily.

Bake crust for 10 minutes.

Meanwhile, in the bowl of the electric mixer, beat the condensed milk, egg yolks, lemon juice, and salt on medium speed for 4 minutes.

Once the crust is done baking, remove from oven and slowly pour the lemon filling over the hot crust as evenly as possible. The crust will be soft since it has only baked for 10 minutes, so if you need to even out the filling, use a small spatula to do so carefully.

Bake 30 minutes and let cool completely in the pan for about 1 to 2 hours.

Refrigerate until the filling is firm, at least 2 hours and up to 2 days.

Using the parchment paper overhang, lift the cake out of the pan onto a cutting board. With a very sharp knife, cut into 12 to 16 squares.

Dust with powdered sugar before serving.

HAYDEN JORDAN

@petitesouthernkitchen

Grace Day

Use this day to pray, rest, and reflect on this week's reading,
giving thanks for the grace that is ours in Christ.

PHILIPPIANS 4:5

Let your graciousness be known
to everyone. The Lord is near.

Scripture is God-breathed and true. When we memorize it, we carry the gospel with us wherever we go.

This week we'll memorize a verse about God's faithfulness, taken from Hannah's prayer of praise on day 32.

Weekly Truth

There is no one holy like the LORD.
There is no one besides you!
And there is no rock like our God.

Find the corresponding memory card in the back of this book.

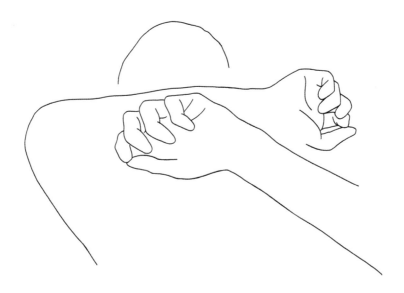

Saul

The First King of Israel

¹ Samuel took the flask of oil, poured it out on Saul's head, kissed him, and said, "Hasn't the LORD anointed you ruler over his inheritance? ² Today when you leave me, you'll find two men at Rachel's Grave at Zelzah in the territory of Benjamin. They will say to you, 'The donkeys you went looking for have been found, and now your father has stopped being concerned about the donkeys and is worried about you, asking: What should I do about my son?'

³ "You will proceed from there until you come to the oak of Tabor. Three men going up to God at Bethel will meet you there, one bringing three goats, one bringing three loaves of bread, and one bringing a clay jar of wine. ⁴ They will ask how you are and give you two loaves of bread, which you will accept from them.

⁵ "After that you will come to Gibeah of God where there are Philistine garrisons. When you arrive at the city, you will meet a group of prophets coming down from the high place prophesying. They will be preceded by harps, tambourines, flutes, and lyres. ⁶ The Spirit of the LORD will come powerfully on you, you will prophesy with them, and you will be transformed. ⁷ When these signs have happened to you, do whatever your circumstances require because God is with you. ⁸ Afterward, go ahead of me to Gilgal. I will come to you to offer burnt offerings and to sacrifice fellowship offerings. Wait seven days until I come to you and show you what to do."

⁹ When Saul turned around to leave Samuel, God changed his heart, and all the signs came about that day. ¹⁰ When Saul and his servant arrived at Gibeah, a group of prophets met him. Then the Spirit of God came powerfully on him, and he prophesied along with them.

¹¹ Everyone who knew him previously and saw him prophesy with the prophets asked each other, "What has happened to the son of Kish? Is Saul also among the prophets?"

¹² Then a man who was from there asked, "And who is their father?"

As a result, "Is Saul also among the prophets?" became a popular saying. ¹³ Then Saul finished prophesying and went to the high place.

¹⁴ Saul's uncle asked him and his servant, "Where did you go?"

"To look for the donkeys," Saul answered. "When we saw they weren't there, we went to Samuel."

¹⁵ "Tell me," Saul's uncle asked, "what did Samuel say to you?"

¹⁶ Saul told him, "He assured us the donkeys had been found." However, Saul did not tell him what Samuel had said about the matter of kingship.

SAUL RECEIVED AS KING

¹⁷ Samuel summoned the people to the LORD at Mizpah ¹⁸ and said to the Israelites, "This is what the LORD, the God of Israel, says: 'I brought Israel out of Egypt, and I rescued you from the power of the Egyptians and all the kingdoms that were oppressing you.' ¹⁹ But today you have rejected your God, who saves you from all your troubles and afflictions. You said to him, 'You must set a king over us.' Now therefore present yourselves before the LORD by your tribes and clans."

²⁰ Samuel had all the tribes of Israel come forward, and the tribe of Benjamin was selected. ²¹ Then he had the tribe of Benjamin come forward by its clans, and the Matrite clan was selected. Finally, Saul son of Kish was selected. But when they searched for him, they could not find him. ²² They again inquired of the LORD, "Has the man come here yet?"

The LORD replied, "There he is, hidden among the supplies."

²³ They ran and got him from there. When he stood among the people, he stood a head taller than anyone else. ²⁴ Samuel said to all the people, "Do you see the one the LORD has chosen? There is no one like him among the entire population."

And all the people shouted, "Long live the king!"

²⁵ Samuel proclaimed to the people the rights of kingship. He wrote them on a scroll, which he placed in the presence of the Lord. Then Samuel sent all the people home.

²⁶ Saul also went to his home in Gibeah, and brave men whose hearts God had touched went with him. ²⁷ But some wicked men said, "How can this guy save us?" They despised him and did not bring him a gift, but Saul said nothing.

1 SAMUEL 13:1–14
SAUL'S FAILURE

¹ Saul was thirty years old when he became king, and he reigned forty-two years over Israel. ² He chose three thousand men from Israel for himself: two thousand were with Saul at Michmash and in Bethel's hill country, and one thousand were with Jonathan in Gibeah of Benjamin. He sent the rest of the troops away, each to his own tent.

³ Jonathan attacked the Philistine garrison that was in Geba, and the Philistines heard about it. So Saul blew the ram's horn throughout the land saying, "Let the Hebrews hear!" ⁴ And all Israel heard the news, "Saul has attacked the Philistine garrison, and Israel is now repulsive to the Philistines." Then the troops were summoned to join Saul at Gilgal.

⁵ The Philistines also gathered to fight against Israel: three thousand chariots, six thousand horsemen, and troops as numerous as the sand on the seashore. They went up and camped at Michmash, east of Beth-aven.

⁶ The men of Israel saw that they were in trouble because the troops were in a difficult situation. They hid in caves, in thickets, among rocks, and in holes and cisterns. ⁷ Some Hebrews even crossed the Jordan to the land of Gad and Gilead.

Saul, however, was still at Gilgal, and all his troops were gripped with fear. ⁸ He waited seven days for the appointed time that Samuel had set, but Samuel didn't come to Gilgal, and the troops were deserting him. ⁹ So Saul said, "Bring me the burnt offering and the fellowship offerings." Then he offered the burnt offering.

¹⁰ Just as he finished offering the burnt offering, Samuel arrived. So Saul went out to greet him, ¹¹ and Samuel asked, "What have you done?"

Saul answered, "When I saw that the troops were deserting me and you didn't come within the appointed days and the Philistines were gathering at Michmash, ¹² I thought, 'The Philistines will now descend on me at Gilgal, and I haven't sought the Lord's favor.' So I forced myself to offer the burnt offering."

¹³ Samuel said to Saul, "You have been foolish. You have not kept the command the Lord your God gave you. It was at this time that the Lord would have permanently established your reign over Israel, ¹⁴ but now your reign will not endure. The Lord has found a man after his own heart, and the Lord has appointed him as ruler over his people, because you have not done what the Lord commanded."

NUMBERS 18:7

"But you and your sons will carry out your priestly responsibilities for everything concerning the altar and for what is inside the curtain, and you will do that work. I am giving you the work of the priesthood as a gift, but an unauthorized person who comes near the sanctuary will be put to death."

1   Summarize the events of
     this story.

2   What stood out to you?
     What questions do you have?

3   What is God teaching you
     in the reading?

David

A Man After God's Own Heart

[1] The LORD said to Samuel, "How long are you going to mourn for Saul, since I have rejected him as king over Israel? Fill your horn with oil and go. I am sending you to Jesse of Bethlehem because I have selected a king from his sons."

[2] Samuel asked, "How can I go? Saul will hear about it and kill me!"

The LORD answered, "Take a young cow with you and say, 'I have come to sacrifice to the LORD.' [3] Then invite Jesse to the sacrifice, and I will let you know what you are to do. You are to anoint for me the one I indicate to you."

[4] Samuel did what the LORD directed and went to Bethlehem. When the elders of the town met him, they trembled and asked, "Do you come in peace?"

[5] "In peace," he replied. "I've come to sacrifice to the LORD. Consecrate yourselves and come with me to the sacrifice." Then he consecrated Jesse and his sons and invited them to the sacrifice. [6] When they arrived, Samuel saw Eliab and said, "Certainly the LORD's anointed one is here before him."

[7] But the LORD said to Samuel, "Do not look at his appearance or his stature because I have rejected him. Humans do not see what the LORD sees, for humans see what is visible, but the LORD sees the heart."

[8] Jesse called Abinadab and presented him to Samuel. "The LORD hasn't chosen this one either," Samuel said. [9] Then Jesse presented Shammah, but Samuel said, "The LORD hasn't chosen this one either." [10] After Jesse presented seven of his sons to him, Samuel told Jesse, "The LORD hasn't chosen any of these." [11] Samuel asked him, "Are these all the sons you have?"

"There is still the youngest," he answered, "but right now he's tending the sheep." Samuel told Jesse, "Send for him. We won't sit down to eat until he gets here." [12] So Jesse sent for him. He had beautiful eyes and a healthy, handsome appearance.

Then the LORD said, "Anoint him, for he is the one." [13] So Samuel took the horn of oil and anointed him in the presence of his brothers, and the Spirit of the LORD came powerfully on David from that day forward. Then Samuel set out and went to Ramah.

[1] All the tribes of Israel came to David at Hebron and said, "Here we are, your own flesh and blood. [2] Even while Saul was king over us, you were the one who led us out to battle

and brought us back. The LORD also said to you, 'You will shepherd my people Israel, and you will be ruler over Israel.'"

3 So all the elders of Israel came to the king at Hebron. King David made a covenant with them at Hebron in the LORD's presence, and they anointed David king over Israel.

4 David was thirty years old when he began his reign; he reigned forty years. 5 In Hebron he reigned over Judah seven years and six months, and in Jerusalem he reigned thirty-three years over all Israel and Judah.

6 The king and his men marched to Jerusalem against the Jebusites who inhabited the land. The Jebusites had said to David: "You will never get in here. Even the blind and lame can repel you" thinking, "David can't get in here."

7 Yet David did capture the stronghold of Zion, that is, the city of David. 8 He said that day, "Whoever attacks the Jebusites must go through the water shaft to reach the lame and the blind who are despised by David." For this reason it is said, "The blind and the lame will never enter the house."

9 David took up residence in the stronghold, which he named the city of David. He built it up all the way around from the supporting terraces inward. 10 David became more and more powerful, and the LORD God of Armies was with him. 11 King Hiram of Tyre sent envoys to David; he also sent cedar logs, carpenters, and stonemasons, and they built a palace for David. 12 Then David knew that the LORD had established him as king over Israel and had exalted his kingdom for the sake of his people Israel.

2 SAMUEL 7
THE LORD'S COVENANT WITH DAVID

1 When the king had settled into his palace and the LORD had given him rest on every side from all his enemies, 2 the king said to the prophet Nathan, "Look, I am living in a cedar house while the ark of God sits inside tent curtains."

3 So Nathan told the king, "Go and do all that is on your mind, for the LORD is with you."

4 But that night the word of the LORD came to Nathan: 5 "Go to my servant David and say, 'This is what the LORD says: Are you to build me a house to dwell in? 6 From the time I brought the Israelites out of Egypt until today I have not dwelt in a house; instead, I have been moving around with a tent as my dwelling. 7 In all my journeys with all the Israelites, have I ever spoken a word to one of the tribes

of Israel, whom I commanded to shepherd my people Israel, asking: Why haven't you built me a house of cedar?'

8 "So now this is what you are to say to my servant David: 'This is what the LORD of Armies says: I took you from the pasture, from tending the flock, to be ruler over my people Israel. 9 I have been with you wherever you have gone, and I have destroyed all your enemies before you. I will make a great name for you like that of the greatest on the earth. 10 I will designate a place for my people Israel and plant them, so that they may live there and not be disturbed again. Evildoers will not continue to oppress them as they have done 11 ever since the day I ordered judges to be over my people Israel. I will give you rest from all your enemies.

"'The LORD declares to you: The LORD himself will make a house for you. 12 When your time comes and you rest with your fathers, I will raise up after you your descendant, who will come from your body, and I will establish his kingdom. 13 He is the one who will build a house for my name, and I will establish the throne of his kingdom forever. 14 I will be his father, and he will be my son. When he does wrong, I will discipline him with a rod of men and blows from mortals. 15 But my faithful love will never leave him as it did when I removed it from Saul, whom I removed from before you. 16 Your house and kingdom will endure before me forever, and your throne will be established forever.'"

17 Nathan reported all these words and this entire vision to David.

DAVID'S PRAYER OF THANKSGIVING

18 Then King David went in, sat in the LORD's presence, and said,

Who am I, Lord GOD, and what is my house that you have brought me this far? 19 What you have done so far was a little thing to you, Lord GOD, for you have also spoken about your servant's house in the distant future. And this is a revelation for mankind, Lord GOD. 20 What more can David say to you? You know your servant, Lord GOD. 21 Because of your word and according to your will, you have revealed all these great things to your servant.

22 This is why you are great, Lord GOD. There is no one like you, and there is no God besides you, as all we have heard confirms. 23 And who is like your people Israel? God came to one nation on earth in order to redeem a people for himself, to make a name for himself, and to perform for them great and awesome acts, driving out nations and their gods before your people you redeemed for yourself from Egypt. 24 You established your people Israel to be your own people forever, and you, LORD, have become their God.

25 Now, LORD God, fulfill the promise forever that you have made to your servant and his house. Do as you have promised, 26 so that your name will be exalted forever, when it is said, "The LORD of Armies is God over Israel." The house of your servant David will be established before you 27 since you, LORD of Armies, God of Israel, have revealed this to your servant when you said, "I will build a house for you." Therefore, your servant has found the courage to pray this prayer to you. 28 Lord GOD, you are God; your words are true, and you have promised this good thing to your servant. 29 Now, please bless your servant's house so that it will continue before you forever. For you, Lord GOD, have spoken, and with your blessing your servant's house will be blessed forever.

ACTS 13:21–23

21 Then they asked for a king, and God gave them Saul the son of Kish, a man of the tribe of Benjamin, for forty years. 22 After removing him, he raised up David as their king and testified about him: "I have found David the son of Jesse to be a man after my own heart, who will carry out all my will."

23 From this man's descendants, as he promised, God brought to Israel the Savior, Jesus.

1 Summarize the events of
   this story.

2 What stood out to you?
   What questions do you have?

3 What is God teaching you
   in the reading?

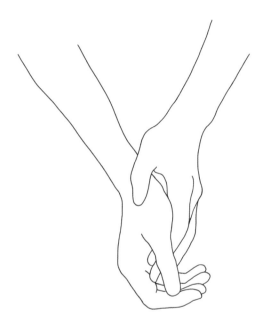

Abigail

A Woman of Discernment and Generosity

¹ Samuel died, and all Israel assembled to mourn for him, and they buried him by his home in Ramah. David then went down to the Wilderness of Paran.

² A man in Maon had a business in Carmel; he was a very rich man with three thousand sheep and one thousand goats and was shearing his sheep in Carmel. ³ The man's name was Nabal, and his wife's name, Abigail. The woman was intelligent and beautiful, but the man, a Calebite, was harsh and evil in his dealings.

⁴ While David was in the wilderness, he heard that Nabal was shearing sheep, ⁵ so David sent ten young men instructing them, "Go up to Carmel, and when you come to Nabal, greet him in my name. ⁶ Then say this: 'Long life to you, and peace to you, peace to your family, and peace to all that is yours. ⁷ I hear that you are shearing. When your shepherds were with us, we did not harass them, and nothing of theirs was missing the whole time they were in Carmel. ⁸ Ask your young men, and they will tell you. So let my young men find favor with you, for we have come on a feast day. Please give whatever you have on hand to your servants and to your son David.'"

⁹ David's young men went and said all these things to Nabal on David's behalf, and they waited. ¹⁰ Nabal asked them, "Who is David? Who is Jesse's son? Many slaves these days are running away from their masters. ¹¹ Am I supposed to take my bread, my water, and my meat that I butchered for my shearers and give them to these men? I don't know where they are from."

¹² David's young men retraced their steps. When they returned to him, they reported all these words. ¹³ He said to his men, "All of you, put on your swords!" So each man put on his sword, and David also put on his sword. About four hundred men followed David while two hundred stayed with the supplies.

¹⁴ One of Nabal's young men informed Abigail, Nabal's wife: "Look, David sent messengers from the wilderness to greet our master, but he screamed at them. ¹⁵ The men treated us very well. When we were in the field, we weren't harassed and nothing of ours was missing the whole time we were living among them. ¹⁶ They were a wall around us, both day and night, the entire time we were with them herding the sheep. ¹⁷ Now consider carefully what you should do, because there is certain to be trouble for our master and his entire family. He is such a worthless fool nobody can talk to him!"

¹⁸ Abigail hurried, taking two hundred loaves of bread, two clay jars of wine, five butchered sheep, a bushel of roasted grain, one hundred clusters of raisins, and two hundred cakes of pressed figs, and loaded them on donkeys. ¹⁹ Then she said to her male servants, "Go ahead of me. I will be right behind you." But she did not tell her husband Nabal.

²⁰ As she rode the donkey down a mountain pass hidden from view, she saw David and his men coming toward her and met them. ²¹ David had just said, "I guarded everything that belonged to this man in the wilderness for nothing. He was not missing anything, yet he paid me back evil for good. ²² May God punish me and do so severely if I let any of his males survive until morning."

²³ When Abigail saw David, she quickly got off the donkey and knelt down with her face to the ground and paid homage to David. ²⁴ She knelt at his feet and said, "The guilt is mine, my lord, but please let your servant speak to you directly. Listen to the words of your servant. ²⁵ My lord should pay no attention to this worthless fool Nabal, for he lives up to his name: His name means 'stupid,' and stupidity is all he knows. I, your servant, didn't see my lord's young men whom you sent. ²⁶ Now my lord, as surely as the Lord lives and as you yourself live— it is the Lord who kept you from participating in bloodshed and avenging yourself by your own hand—may your enemies and those who intend to harm my lord be like Nabal. ²⁷ Let this gift your servant has brought to my lord be given to the young men who follow my lord. ²⁸ Please forgive your servant's offense, for the Lord is certain to make a lasting dynasty for my lord because he fights the Lord's battles. Throughout your life, may evil not be found in you.

²⁹ "Someone is pursuing you and intends to take your life. My lord's life is tucked safely in the place where the Lord

Then David said to Abigail, "Blessed be the LORD God of Israel, who sent you to meet me today!"

your God protects the living, but he is flinging away your enemies' lives like stones from a sling. 30 When the LORD does for my lord all the good he promised you and appoints you ruler over Israel, 31 there will not be remorse or a troubled conscience for my lord because of needless bloodshed or my lord's revenge. And when the LORD does good things for my lord, may you remember me your servant."

32 Then David said to Abigail, "Blessed be the LORD God of Israel, who sent you to meet me today! 33 May your discernment be blessed, and may you be blessed. Today you kept me from participating in bloodshed and avenging myself by my own hand. 34 Otherwise, as surely as the LORD God of Israel lives, who prevented me from harming you, if you had not come quickly to meet me, Nabal wouldn't have had any males left by morning light." 35 Then David accepted what she had brought him and said, "Go home in peace. See, I have heard what you said and have granted your request."

36 Then Abigail went to Nabal, and there he was in his house, holding a feast fit for a king. Nabal's heart was cheerful, and he was very drunk, so she didn't say anything to him until morning light.

37 In the morning when Nabal sobered up, his wife told him about these events. His heart died and he became a stone. 38 About ten days later, the LORD struck Nabal dead.

39 When David heard that Nabal was dead, he said, "Blessed be the LORD who championed my cause against Nabal's insults and restrained his servant from doing evil. The LORD brought Nabal's evil deeds back on his own head."

Then David sent messengers to speak to Abigail about marrying him. 40 When David's servants came to Abigail at Carmel, they said to her, "David sent us to bring you to him as a wife."

41 She stood up, paid homage with her face to the ground, and said, "Here I am, your servant, a slave to wash the feet of my lord's servants." 42 Then Abigail got up quickly, and with her five female servants accompanying her, rode on the donkey following David's messengers. And so she became his wife.

43 David also married Ahinoam of Jezreel, and the two of them became his wives. 44 But Saul gave his daughter Michal, David's wife, to Palti son of Laish, who was from Gallim.

PROVERBS 15:1–4

1 A gentle answer turns away anger,
but a harsh word stirs up wrath.

2 The tongue of the wise makes knowledge attractive,
but the mouth of fools blurts out foolishness.

3 The eyes of the LORD are everywhere,
observing the wicked and the good.

4 The tongue that heals is a tree of life,
but a devious tongue breaks the spirit.

1 Summarize the events of
   this story.

2 What stood out to you?
   What questions do you have?

3 What is God teaching you
   in the reading?

Bathsheba

Wife of Uriah and Mother of Solomon

2 SAMUEL 11:1–17, 26–27

DAVID'S ADULTERY WITH BATHSHEBA

¹ In the spring when kings march out to war, David sent Joab with his officers and all Israel. They destroyed the Ammonites and besieged Rabbah, but David remained in Jerusalem.

² One evening David got up from his bed and strolled around on the roof of the palace. From the roof he saw a woman bathing—a very beautiful woman. ³ So David sent someone to inquire about her, and he said, "Isn't this Bathsheba, daughter of Eliam and wife of Uriah the Hethite?"

⁴ David sent messengers to get her, and when she came to him, he slept with her. Now she had just been purifying herself from her uncleanness. Afterward, she returned home. ⁵ The woman conceived and sent word to inform David: "I am pregnant."

⁶ David sent orders to Joab: "Send me Uriah the Hethite." So Joab sent Uriah to David. ⁷ When Uriah came to him, David asked how Joab and the troops were doing and how the war was going. ⁸ Then he said to Uriah, "Go down to your house and wash your feet." So Uriah left the palace, and a gift from the king followed him. ⁹ But Uriah slept at the door of the palace with all his master's servants; he did not go down to his house.

¹⁰ When it was reported to David, "Uriah didn't go home," David questioned Uriah, "Haven't you just come from a journey? Why didn't you go home?"

¹¹ Uriah answered David, "The ark, Israel, and Judah are dwelling in tents, and my master Joab and his soldiers are camping in the open field. How can I enter my house to eat and drink and sleep with my wife? As surely as you live and by your life, I will not do this!"

¹² "Stay here today also," David said to Uriah, "and tomorrow I will send you back." So Uriah stayed in Jerusalem that day and the next. ¹³ Then David invited Uriah to eat and drink with him, and David got him drunk. He went out in the evening to lie down on his cot with his master's servants, but he did not go home.

URIAH'S DEATH ARRANGED

¹⁴ The next morning David wrote a letter to Joab and sent it with Uriah. ¹⁵ In the letter he wrote:

> Put Uriah at the front of the fiercest fighting, then withdraw from him so that he is struck down and dies.

¹⁶ When Joab was besieging the city, he put Uriah in the place where he knew the best enemy soldiers were. ¹⁷ Then the men of the city came out and attacked Joab, and some of the men from David's soldiers fell in battle; Uriah the Hethite also died.

…

26 When Uriah's wife heard that her husband Uriah had died, she mourned for him. 27 When the time of mourning ended, David had her brought to his house. She became his wife and bore him a son. However, the LORD considered what David had done to be evil.

2 SAMUEL 12:7–25

7 Nathan replied to David, "You are the man! This is what the LORD God of Israel says: 'I anointed you king over Israel, and I rescued you from Saul. 8 I gave your master's house to you and your master's wives into your arms, and I gave you the house of Israel and Judah, and if that was not enough, I would have given you even more. 9 Why then have you despised the LORD's command by doing what I consider evil? You struck down Uriah the Hethite with the sword and took his wife as your own wife—you murdered him with the Ammonite's sword. 10 Now therefore, the sword will never leave your house because you despised me and took the wife of Uriah the Hethite to be your own wife.'

11 "This is what the LORD says, 'I am going to bring disaster on you from your own family: I will take your wives and give them to another before your very eyes, and he will sleep with them in broad daylight. 12 You acted in secret, but I will do this before all Israel and in broad daylight.'"

13 David responded to Nathan, "I have sinned against the LORD."

Then Nathan replied to David, "And the LORD has taken away your sin; you will not die. 14 However, because you treated the LORD with such contempt in this matter, the son born to you will die." 15 Then Nathan went home.

THE DEATH OF BATHSHEBA'S SON

The LORD struck the baby that Uriah's wife had borne to David, and he became deathly ill. 16 David pleaded with God for the boy. He fasted, went home, and spent the night lying on the ground. 17 The elders of his house stood beside him to get him up from the ground, but he was unwilling and would not eat anything with them.

18 On the seventh day the baby died. But David's servants were afraid to tell him the baby was dead. They said, "Look, while the baby was alive, we spoke to him, and he wouldn't listen to us. So how can we tell him the baby is dead? He may do something desperate."

19 When David saw that his servants were whispering to each other, he guessed that the baby was dead. So he asked his servants, "Is the baby dead?"

"He is dead," they replied.

20 Then David got up from the ground. He washed, anointed himself, changed his clothes, went to the LORD's house, and worshiped. Then he went home and requested something to eat. So they served him food, and he ate.

21 His servants asked him, "Why have you done this? While the baby was alive, you fasted and wept, but when he died, you got up and ate food."

22 He answered, "While the baby was alive, I fasted and wept because I thought, 'Who knows? The LORD may be gracious to me and let him live.' 23 But now that he is dead, why should I fast? Can I bring him back again? I'll go to him, but he will never return to me."

THE BIRTH OF SOLOMON

24 Then David comforted his wife Bathsheba; he went to her and slept with her. She gave birth to a son and named him Solomon. The LORD loved him, 25 and he sent a message through the prophet Nathan, who named him Jedidiah, because of the LORD.

1 KINGS 1:1a, 5–31
DAVID'S LAST DAYS

1 Now King David was old and advanced in age.

...

ADONIJAH'S BID FOR POWER

5 Adonijah son of Haggith kept exalting himself, saying, "I will be king!" He prepared chariots, cavalry, and fifty men to run ahead of him. 6 But his father had never once infuriated him by asking, "Why did you do that?" In addition, he was quite handsome and was born after Absalom. 7 He conspired with Joab son of Zeruiah and with the priest Abiathar. They

supported Adonijah, [8] but the priest Zadok, Benaiah son of Jehoiada, the prophet Nathan, Shimei, Rei, and David's royal guard did not side with Adonijah.

[9] Adonijah sacrificed sheep, goats, cattle, and fattened cattle near the stone of Zoheleth, which is next to En-rogel. He invited all his royal brothers and all the men of Judah, the servants of the king, [10] but he did not invite the prophet Nathan, Benaiah, the royal guard, or his brother Solomon.

NATHAN'S AND BATHSHEBA'S APPEALS

[11] Then Nathan said to Bathsheba, Solomon's mother, "Have you not heard that Adonijah son of Haggith has become king and our lord David does not know it? [12] Now please come and let me advise you. Save your life and the life of your son Solomon. [13] Go, approach King David and say to him, 'My lord the king, did you not swear to your servant: Your son Solomon is to become king after me, and he is the one who is to sit on my throne? So why has Adonijah become king?' [14] At that moment, while you are still there speaking with the king, I'll come in after you and confirm your words."

[15] So Bathsheba went to the king in his bedroom. Since the king was very old, Abishag the Shunammite was attending to him. [16] Bathsheba knelt low and paid homage to the king, and he asked, "What do you want?"

[17] She replied, "My lord, you swore to your servant by the LORD your God, 'Your son Solomon is to become king after me, and he is the one who is to sit on my throne.' [18] Now look, Adonijah has become king. And, my lord the king, you didn't know it. [19] He has lavishly sacrificed oxen, fattened cattle, and sheep. He invited all the king's sons, the priest Abiathar, and Joab the commander of the army, but he did not invite your servant Solomon. [20] Now, my lord the king, the eyes of all Israel are on you to tell them who will sit on the throne of my lord the king after him. [21] Otherwise, when my lord the king rests with his fathers, I and my son Solomon will be regarded as criminals."

[22] At that moment, while she was still speaking with the king, the prophet Nathan arrived, [23] and it was announced to the king, "The prophet Nathan is here." He came into the king's presence and paid homage to him with his face to the ground.

[24] "My lord the king," Nathan said, "did you say, 'Adonijah is to become king after me, and he is the one who is to sit on my throne'? [25] For today he went down and lavishly sacrificed oxen, fattened cattle, and sheep. He invited all the sons of the king, the commanders of the army, and the priest Abiathar. And look! They're eating and drinking in his presence, and they're saying, 'Long live King Adonijah!' [26] But he did not invite me—me, your servant—or the priest Zadok or Benaiah son of Jehoiada or your servant Solomon. [27] I'm certain my lord the king would not have let this happen without letting your servant know who will sit on my lord the king's throne after him."

SOLOMON CONFIRMED KING

[28] King David responded by saying, "Call in Bathsheba for me." So she came into the king's presence and stood before him. [29] The king swore an oath and said, "As the LORD lives, who has redeemed my life from every difficulty, [30] just as I swore to you by the LORD God of Israel: Your son Solomon is to become king after me, and he is the one who is to sit on my throne in my place, that is exactly what I will do this very day."

[31] Bathsheba knelt low with her face to the ground, paying homage to the king, and said, "May my lord King David live forever!"

1 Summarize the events of
   this story.

2 What stood out to you?
   What questions do you have?

3 What is God teaching you
   in the reading?

Tamar

A Beautiful Woman Made Desolate

2 SAMUEL 13:1–21

AMNON RAPES TAMAR

¹ Some time passed. David's son Absalom had a beautiful sister named Tamar, and David's son Amnon was infatuated with her. ² Amnon was frustrated to the point of making himself sick over his sister Tamar because she was a virgin, but it seemed impossible to do anything to her. ³ Amnon had a friend named Jonadab, a son of David's brother Shimeah. Jonadab was a very shrewd man, ⁴ and he asked Amnon, "Why are you, the king's son, so miserable every morning? Won't you tell me?"

Amnon replied, "I'm in love with Tamar, my brother Absalom's sister."

⁵ Jonadab said to him, "Lie down on your bed and pretend you're sick. When your father comes to see you, say to him, 'Please let my sister Tamar come and give me something to eat. Let her prepare a meal in my presence so I can watch and eat from her hand.'"

⁶ So Amnon lay down and pretended to be sick. When the king came to see him, Amnon said to him, "Please let my sister Tamar come and make a couple of cakes in my presence so I can eat from her hand."

⁷ David sent word to Tamar at the palace: "Please go to your brother Amnon's house and prepare a meal for him."

⁸ Then Tamar went to his house while Amnon was lying down. She took dough, kneaded it, made cakes in his presence, and baked them. ⁹ She brought the pan and set it down in front of him, but he refused to eat. Amnon said, "Everyone leave me!" And everyone left him. ¹⁰ "Bring the meal to the bedroom," Amnon told Tamar, "so I can eat from your hand." Tamar took the cakes she had made and went to her

brother Amnon's bedroom. [11] When she brought them to him to eat, he grabbed her and said, "Come sleep with me, my sister!"

[12] "Don't, my brother!" she cried. "Don't disgrace me, for such a thing should never be done in Israel. Don't commit this outrage! [13] Where could I ever go with my humiliation? And you—you would be like one of the outrageous fools in Israel! Please, speak to the king, for he won't keep me from you." [14] But he refused to listen to her, and because he was stronger than she was, he disgraced her by raping her.

[15] So Amnon hated Tamar with such intensity that the hatred he hated her with was greater than the love he had loved her with. "Get out of here!" he said.

[16] "No," she cried, "sending me away is much worse than the great wrong you've already done to me!"

But he refused to listen to her. [17] Instead, he called to the servant who waited on him: "Get this away from me, throw her out, and bolt the door behind her!" [18] Amnon's servant threw her out and bolted the door behind her. Now Tamar was wearing a long-sleeved garment, because this is what the king's virgin daughters wore. [19] Tamar put ashes on her head and tore the long-sleeved garment she was wearing. She put her hand on her head and went away crying out.

[20] Her brother Absalom said to her: "Has your brother Amnon been with you? Be quiet for now, my sister. He is your brother. Don't take this thing to heart." So Tamar lived as a desolate woman in the house of her brother Absalom.

[21] When King David heard about all these things, he was furious.

PSALM 55

[1] God, listen to my prayer
and do not hide from my plea for help.
[2] Pay attention to me and answer me.
I am restless and in turmoil with my complaint,
[3] because of the enemy's words,
because of the pressure of the wicked.
For they bring down disaster on me
and harass me in anger.

[4] My heart shudders within me;
terrors of death sweep over me.
[5] Fear and trembling grip me;

Cast your burden on the LORD, and he will sustain you; he will never allow the righteous to be shaken.

horror has overwhelmed me.
⁶ I said, "If only I had wings like a dove!
I would fly away and find rest.
⁷ How far away I would flee;
I would stay in the wilderness. *Selah*
⁸ I would hurry to my shelter
from the raging wind and the storm."

⁹ Lord, confuse and confound their speech,
for I see violence and strife in the city;
¹⁰ day and night they make the rounds on its walls.
Crime and trouble are within it;
¹¹ destruction is inside it;
oppression and deceit never leave its marketplace.

¹² Now it is not an enemy who insults me—
otherwise I could bear it;
it is not a foe who rises up against me—
otherwise I could hide from him.
¹³ But it is you, a man who is my peer,
my companion and good friend!
¹⁴ We used to have close fellowship;
we walked with the crowd into the house of God.

¹⁵ Let death take them by surprise;
let them go down to Sheol alive,
because evil is in their homes and within them.
¹⁶ But I call to God,
and the LORD will save me.
¹⁷ I complain and groan morning, noon, and night,
and he hears my voice.
¹⁸ Though many are against me,
he will redeem me from my battle unharmed.
¹⁹ God, the one enthroned from long ago,
will hear and will humiliate them *Selah*
because they do not change
and do not fear God.

²⁰ My friend acts violently
against those at peace with him;
he violates his covenant.
²¹ His buttery words are smooth,
but war is in his heart.
His words are softer than oil,
but they are drawn swords.

²² Cast your burden on the LORD,
and he will sustain you;
he will never allow the righteous to be shaken.

²³ God, you will bring them down
to the Pit of destruction;
men of bloodshed and treachery
will not live out half their days.
But I will trust in you.

1   Summarize the events of
    this story.

2   What stood out to you?
    What questions do you have?

3   What is God teaching you
    in the reading?

Bruschetta Chicken Pizza

PREP TIME	BAKE TIME	SERVES
15 minutes	15 minutes	10

AIMEE MARS

@aimeemarsliving

INGREDIENTS

1 chicken breast

½ teaspoon Italian seasoning

Salt and pepper

2 plum tomatoes, diced

¼ red onion, chopped finely

⅛ cup fresh basil or parsley, shredded

1 tablespoon olive oil

1 pie crust (frozen, prepared, or homemade)

1–2 tablespoons olive oil + more for crust

6 ounces fresh mozzarella cheese

½ cup balsamic vinegar

3 teaspoons brown sugar

1 ounce parmesan cheese

INSTRUCTIONS

Heat olive oil in a medium skillet over medium-high heat and season both sides of the chicken with the Italian seasoning and salt and pepper. Add the chicken to the prepared skillet and cook on each side for 6 to 7 minutes, or until the internal temperature reaches 160°F.

While the chicken is cooking, chop the tomatoes, onion, and basil and place in a medium bowl. Add olive oil and salt and pepper, then toss to coat evenly to finish the bruschetta mixture. Remove chicken from skillet and shred with two forks.

Preheat oven to 450°F. Brush pie crust with olive oil. Tear mozzarella cheese into pieces and arrange on the crust. Top with shredded chicken then sprinkle on the bruschetta mixture. Place the pizza in the oven and cook for 15 to 18 minutes, or until cheese bubbles up and is melted.

Whisk the balsamic vinegar and brown sugar together in a small saucepan and bring to a boil over high heat. Allow mixture to boil for 1 minute, then turn heat to low and simmer for an additional 5 to 7 minutes, or until the vinegar begins to thicken. Set aside.

Once the pizza is cooked, remove from the oven and pour the balsamic glaze on top, then sprinkle with parmesan cheese.

Grace Day

Use this day to pray, rest, and reflect on this week's reading,
giving thanks for the grace that is ours in Christ.

Cast your burden on the LORD,
and he will sustain you:
he will never allow the righteous
to be shaken.

Scripture is God-breathed and true. When we memorize it, we carry the gospel with us wherever we go.

This week we'll memorize 1 Samuel 16:7, a verse from David's story about what God sees and values.

Weekly Truth

1 SAMUEL 16:7

"Humans do not see what the LORD sees, for humans see what is visible, but the LORD sees the heart."

Find the corresponding memory card in the back of this book.

Mephibosheth

Recipient of the King's Kindness

2 SAMUEL 4:4

Saul's son Jonathan had a son whose feet were crippled. He was five years old when the report about Saul and Jonathan came from Jezreel. His nanny picked him up and fled, but as she was hurrying to flee, he fell and became lame. His name was Mephibosheth.

2 SAMUEL 9

DAVID'S KINDNESS TO MEPHIBOSHETH

[1] David asked, "Is there anyone remaining from the family of Saul I can show kindness to for Jonathan's sake?" [2] There was a servant of Saul's family named Ziba. They summoned him to David, and the king said to him, "Are you Ziba?"

"I am your servant," he replied.

[3] So the king asked, "Is there anyone left of Saul's family that I can show the kindness of God to?"

Ziba said to the king, "There is still Jonathan's son who was injured in both feet."

[4] The king asked him, "Where is he?"

Ziba answered the king, "You'll find him in Lo-debar at the house of Machir son of Ammiel." [5] So King David had him brought from the house of Machir son of Ammiel in Lo-debar.

[6] Mephibosheth son of Jonathan son of Saul came to David, fell facedown, and paid homage. David said, "Mephibosheth!"

"I am your servant," he replied.

[7] "Don't be afraid," David said to him, "since I intend to show you kindness for the sake of your father Jonathan. I will restore to you all your grandfather Saul's fields, and you will always eat meals at my table."

[8] Mephibosheth paid homage and said, "What is your servant that you take an interest in a dead dog like me?"

[9] Then the king summoned Saul's attendant Ziba and said to him, "I have given to your master's grandson all that belonged to Saul and his family. [10] You, your sons, and your servants are to work the ground for him, and you are to bring in the crops so your master's grandson will have food to eat. But Mephibosheth, your master's grandson, is always to eat at my table." Now Ziba had fifteen sons and twenty servants.

[11] Ziba said to the king, "Your servant will do all my lord the king commands."

So Mephibosheth ate at David's table just like one of the king's sons. [12] Mephibosheth had a young son whose name was Mica. All those living in Ziba's house were Mephibosheth's servants. [13] However, Mephibosheth lived in Jerusalem because he always ate at the king's table. His feet had been injured.

2 SAMUEL 19:14–30

[14] So he won over all the men of Judah, and they unanimously sent word to the king: "Come back, you and all your servants." [15] Then the king returned. When he arrived at the Jordan, Judah came to Gilgal to meet the king and escort him across the Jordan.

[16] Shimei son of Gera, the Benjaminite from Bahurim, hurried down with the men of Judah to meet King David. [17] There were a thousand men from Benjamin with him. Ziba, an attendant from the house of Saul, with his fifteen sons and twenty servants also rushed down to the Jordan ahead of the king. [18] They forded the Jordan to bring the king's household across and do whatever the king desired.

When Shimei son of Gera crossed the Jordan, he fell facedown before the king [19] and said to him, "My lord, don't hold me guilty, and don't remember your servant's wrongdoing on the day my lord the king left Jerusalem. May the king not take it to heart. [20] For your servant knows that I have sinned. But look! Today I am the first one of the entire house of Joseph to come down to meet my lord the king."

[21] Abishai son of Zeruiah asked, "Shouldn't Shimei be put to death for this, because he cursed the LORD's anointed?"

[22] David answered, "Sons of Zeruiah, do we agree on anything? Have you become my adversary today? Should any man be killed in Israel today? Am I not aware that today I'm king over Israel?" [23] So the king said to Shimei, "You will not die." Then the king gave him his oath.

[24] Mephibosheth, Saul's grandson, also went down to meet the king. He had not taken care of his feet, trimmed his mustache, or washed his clothes from the day the king left until the day he returned safely. [25] When he came from Jerusalem to meet the king, the king asked him, "Mephibosheth, why didn't you come with me?"

[26] "My lord the king," he replied, "my servant Ziba betrayed me. Actually your servant said: 'I'll saddle the donkey for myself so that I may ride it and go with the king'—for your servant is lame. [27] Ziba slandered your servant to my lord the king. But my lord the king is like the angel of God, so do whatever you think best. [28] For my grandfather's entire family deserves death from my lord the king, but you set your servant among those who eat at your table. So what further right do I have to keep on making appeals to the king?"

[29] The king said to him, "Why keep on speaking about these matters of yours? I hereby declare: you and Ziba are to divide the land."

[30] Mephibosheth said to the king, "Instead, since my lord the king has come to his palace safely, let Ziba take it all!"

LUKE 14:12–14 NIV

[12] Then Jesus said to his host, "When you give a luncheon or dinner, do not invite your friends, your brothers or sisters, your relatives, or your rich neighbors; if you do, they may invite you back and so you will be repaid. [13] But when you give a banquet, invite the poor, the crippled, the lame, the blind, [14] and you will be blessed. Although they cannot repay you, you will be repaid at the resurrection of the righteous."

1   Summarize the events of
    this story.

2   What stood out to you?
    What questions do you have?

3   What is God teaching you
    in the reading?

Solomon

Wise Like No Other

THE LORD APPEARS TO SOLOMON

¹ Solomon made an alliance with Pharaoh king of Egypt by marrying Pharaoh's daughter. Solomon brought her to the city of David until he finished building his palace, the Lord's temple, and the wall surrounding Jerusalem. ² However, the people were sacrificing on the high places, because until that time a temple for the Lord's name had not been built. ³ Solomon loved the Lord by walking in the statutes of his father David, but he also sacrificed and burned incense on the high places.

⁴ The king went to Gibeon to sacrifice there because it was the most famous high place. He offered a thousand burnt offerings on that altar. ⁵ At Gibeon the Lord appeared to Solomon in a dream at night. God said, "Ask. What should I give you?"

⁶ And Solomon replied, "You have shown great and faithful love to your servant, my father David, because he walked before you in faithfulness, righteousness, and integrity. You have continued this great and faithful love for him by giving him a son to sit on his throne, as it is today.

⁷ "Lord my God, you have now made your servant king in my father David's place. Yet I am just a youth with no experience in leadership. ⁸ Your servant is among your people you have chosen, a people too many to be numbered or counted. ⁹ So give your servant a receptive heart to judge your people and to discern between good and evil. For who is able to judge this great people of yours?"

¹⁰ Now it pleased the Lord that Solomon had requested this. ¹¹ So God said to him, "Because you have requested this and did not ask for long life or riches for yourself, or the death of your enemies, but you asked discernment for yourself to administer justice, ¹² I will therefore do what you have asked. I will give you a wise and understanding heart, so that there has never been anyone like you before and never will be again. ¹³ In addition, I will give you what you did not ask for: both riches and honor, so that no king will be your equal during your entire life. ¹⁴ If you walk in my ways and keep my statutes and commands just as your father David did, I will give you a long life."

¹⁵ Then Solomon woke up and realized it had been a dream. He went to Jerusalem, stood before the ark of the Lord's covenant, and offered burnt offerings and fellowship offerings. Then he held a feast for all his servants.

SOLOMON'S WISDOM

¹⁶ Then two women who were prostitutes came to the king and stood before him. ¹⁷ One woman said, "Please, my lord, this woman and I live in the same house, and I had a baby while she was in the house. ¹⁸ On the third day after I gave birth, she also had a baby and we were alone. No one else was

with us in the house; just the two of us were there. [19] During the night this woman's son died because she lay on him. [20] She got up in the middle of the night and took my son from my side while your servant was asleep. She laid him in her arms, and she put her dead son in my arms. [21] When I got up in the morning to nurse my son, I discovered he was dead. That morning, when I looked closely at him I realized that he was not the son I gave birth to."

[22] "No," the other woman said. "My son is the living one; your son is the dead one."

The first woman said, "No, your son is the dead one; my son is the living one." So they argued before the king.

[23] The king replied, "This woman says, 'This is my son who is alive, and your son is dead,' but that woman says, 'No, your son is dead, and my son is alive.'" [24] The king continued, "Bring me a sword." So they brought the sword to the king. [25] And the king said, "Cut the living boy in two and give half to one and half to the other."

[26] The woman whose son was alive spoke to the king because she felt great compassion for her son. "My lord, give her the living baby," she said, "but please don't have him killed!"

But the other one said, "He will not be mine or yours. Cut him in two!"

[27] The king responded, "Give the living baby to the first woman, and don't kill him. She is his mother." [28] All Israel heard about the judgment the king had given, and they stood in awe of the king because they saw that God's wisdom was in him to carry out justice.

1 KINGS 8:54–66
SOLOMON'S BLESSING

[54] When Solomon finished praying this entire prayer and petition to the LORD, he got up from kneeling before the altar of the LORD, with his hands spread out toward heaven, [55] and he stood and blessed the whole congregation of Israel with a loud voice: [56] "Blessed be the LORD! He has given rest to his people Israel according to all he has said. Not one of all the good promises he made through his servant Moses has failed. [57] May the LORD our God be with us as he was with our ancestors. May he not abandon us or leave us [58] so that he causes us to be devoted to him, to walk in all his ways, and to keep his commands, statutes, and ordinances, which he commanded our ancestors. [59] May my words with which I have made my petition before the LORD be near the LORD our God day and night. May he uphold his servant's cause and the cause of his people Israel, as each day requires. [60] May all the peoples of the earth know that the LORD is God. There is no other! [61] Be wholeheartedly devoted

to the LORD our God to walk in his statutes and to keep his commands, as it is today."

⁶² The king and all Israel with him were offering sacrifices in the LORD's presence. ⁶³ Solomon offered a sacrifice of fellowship offerings to the LORD: twenty-two thousand cattle and one hundred twenty thousand sheep and goats. In this manner the king and all the Israelites dedicated the LORD's temple.

⁶⁴ On the same day, the king consecrated the middle of the courtyard that was in front of the LORD's temple because that was where he offered the burnt offering, the grain offering, and the fat of the fellowship offerings since the bronze altar before the LORD was too small to accommodate the burnt offerings, the grain offerings, and the fat of the fellowship offerings.

⁶⁵ Solomon and all Israel with him—a great assembly, from the entrance of Hamath to the Brook of Egypt—observed the festival at that time in the presence of the LORD our God, seven days, and seven more days—fourteen days. ⁶⁶ On the fifteenth day he sent the people away. So they blessed the king and went to their homes rejoicing and with happy hearts for all the goodness that the LORD had done for his servant David and for his people Israel.

1 KINGS 9:1–9
THE LORD'S RESPONSE

¹ When Solomon finished building the temple of the LORD, the royal palace, and all that Solomon desired to do, ² the LORD appeared to Solomon a second time just as he had appeared to him at Gibeon. ³ The LORD said to him:

I have heard your prayer and petition you have made before me. I have consecrated this temple you have built, to put my name there forever; my eyes and my heart will be there at all times.

⁴ As for you, if you walk before me as your father David walked, with a heart of integrity and in what is right, doing everything I have commanded you, and if you keep my statutes and ordinances, ⁵ I will establish your royal throne over Israel forever, as I promised your father David: You will never fail to have a man on the throne of Israel.

⁶ If you or your sons turn away from following me and do not keep my commands—my statutes that I have set before you—and if you go and serve other gods and bow in worship to them, ⁷ I will cut off Israel from the land I gave them, and I will reject the temple I have sanctified for my name. Israel will become an object of scorn and ridicule among all the peoples. ⁸ Though this temple is now exalted, everyone who passes by will be appalled and will scoff. They will say: Why did the LORD do this to this land and this temple? ⁹ Then they will say: Because they abandoned the LORD their God who brought their ancestors out of the land of Egypt. They held on to other gods and bowed in worship to them and served them. Because of this, the LORD brought all this ruin on them.

JAMES 3:13–18
THE WISDOM FROM ABOVE

¹³ Who among you is wise and understanding? By his good conduct he should show that his works are done in the gentleness that comes from wisdom. ¹⁴ But if you have bitter envy and selfish ambition in your heart, don't boast and deny the truth. ¹⁵ Such wisdom does not come down from above but is earthly, unspiritual, demonic. ¹⁶ For where there is envy and selfish ambition, there is disorder and every evil practice. ¹⁷ But the wisdom from above is first pure, then peace-loving, gentle, compliant, full of mercy and good fruits, unwavering, without pretense. ¹⁸ And the fruit of righteousness is sown in peace by those who cultivate peace.

1 Summarize the events of
   this story.

2 What stood out to you?
   What questions do you have?

3 What is God teaching you
   in the reading?

Ahab and Jezebel

The King and Queen of Idolatry

1 KINGS 16:29–33
ISRAEL'S KING AHAB

²⁹ Ahab son of Omri became king over Israel in the thirty-eighth year of Judah's King Asa; Ahab son of Omri reigned over Israel in Samaria twenty-two years. ³⁰ But Ahab son of Omri did what was evil in the LORD's sight more than all who were before him. ³¹ Then, as if following the sin of Jeroboam son of Nebat were not enough, he married Jezebel, the daughter of Ethbaal king of the Sidonians, and then proceeded to serve Baal and bow in worship to him. ³² He set up an altar for Baal in the temple of Baal that he had built in Samaria. ³³ Ahab also made an Asherah pole. Ahab did more to anger the LORD God of Israel than all the kings of Israel who were before him.

1 KINGS 18:1–6
ELIJAH'S MESSAGE TO AHAB

¹ After a long time, the word of the LORD came to Elijah in the third year: "Go and present yourself to Ahab. I will send rain on the surface of the land." ² So Elijah went to present himself to Ahab.

The famine was severe in Samaria. ³ Ahab called for Obadiah, who was in charge of the palace. Obadiah was a man who greatly feared the LORD ⁴ and took a hundred prophets and hid them, fifty men to a cave, and provided them with food and water when Jezebel slaughtered the LORD's prophets.

⁵ Ahab said to Obadiah, "Go throughout the land to every spring and to every wadi. Perhaps we'll find grass so we can keep the horses and mules alive and not have to destroy any cattle." ⁶ They divided the land between them in order to cover it. Ahab went one way by himself, and Obadiah went the other way by himself.

1 KINGS 19:1–5
ELIJAH'S JOURNEY TO HOREB

¹ Ahab told Jezebel everything that Elijah had done and how he had killed all the prophets with the sword. ² So Jezebel sent a messenger to Elijah, saying, "May the gods punish me and do so severely if I don't make your life like the life of one of them by this time tomorrow!"

³ Then Elijah became afraid and immediately ran for his life. When he came to Beer-sheba that belonged to Judah, he left his servant there, ⁴ but he went on a day's journey into the wilderness. He sat down under a broom tree and prayed that he might die. He said, "I have had enough! LORD, take my life, for I'm no better than my fathers." ⁵ Then he lay down and slept under the broom tree.

Suddenly, an angel touched him. The angel told him, "Get up and eat."

AHAB AND NABOTH'S VINEYARD

¹ Some time passed after these events. Naboth the Jezreelite had a vineyard; it was in Jezreel next to the palace of King Ahab of Samaria. ² So Ahab spoke to Naboth, saying, "Give me your vineyard so I can have it for a vegetable garden, since it is right next to my palace. I will give you a better vineyard in its place, or if you prefer, I will give you its value in silver."

³ But Naboth said to Ahab, "I will never give my fathers' inheritance to you."

⁴ So Ahab went to his palace resentful and angry because of what Naboth the Jezreelite had told him. He had said, "I will not give you my fathers' inheritance." He lay down on his bed, turned his face away, and didn't eat any food.

⁵ Then his wife Jezebel came to him and said to him, "Why are you so upset that you refuse to eat?"

⁶ "Because I spoke to Naboth the Jezreelite," he replied. "I told him: Give me your vineyard for silver, or if you wish, I will give you a vineyard in its place. But he said, 'I won't give you my vineyard!'"

⁷ Then his wife Jezebel said to him, "Now, exercise your royal power over Israel. Get up, eat some food, and be happy. For I will give you the vineyard of Naboth the Jezreelite." ⁸ So she wrote letters in Ahab's name and sealed them with his seal. She sent the letters to the elders and nobles who lived with Naboth in his city. ⁹ In the letters, she wrote:

> Proclaim a fast and seat Naboth at the head of the people. ¹⁰ Then seat two wicked men opposite him and have them testify against him, saying, "You have cursed God and the king!" Then take him out and stone him to death.

¹¹ The men of his city, the elders and nobles who lived in his city, did as Jezebel had sent word to them, just as it was written in the letters she had sent them. ¹² They proclaimed a fast and seated Naboth at the head of the people. ¹³ The two wicked men came in and sat opposite him. Then the wicked men testified against Naboth in the presence of the people, saying, "Naboth has cursed God and the king!" So they took him outside the city and stoned him to death with stones. ¹⁴ Then they sent word to Jezebel: "Naboth has been stoned to death."

¹⁵ When Jezebel heard that Naboth had been stoned to death, she said to Ahab, "Get up and take possession of the vineyard of Naboth the Jezreelite who refused to give it to you for silver, since Naboth isn't alive, but dead." ¹⁶ When Ahab heard that Naboth was dead, he got up to go down to the vineyard of Naboth the Jezreelite to take possession of it.

"Be on your guard against false prophets who come to you in sheep's clothing but inwardly are ravaging wolves."

THE LORD'S JUDGMENT ON AHAB

¹⁷ Then the word of the LORD came to Elijah the Tishbite: ¹⁸ "Get up and go to meet King Ahab of Israel, who is in Samaria. He's in Naboth's vineyard, where he has gone to take possession of it. ¹⁹ Tell him, 'This is what the LORD says: Have you murdered and also taken possession?' Then tell him, 'This is what the LORD says: In the place where the dogs licked up Naboth's blood, the dogs will also lick up your blood!'"

²⁰ Ahab said to Elijah, "So, my enemy, you've found me, have you?"

He replied, "I have found you because you devoted yourself to do what is evil in the LORD's sight. ²¹ This is what the LORD says: 'I am about to bring disaster on you and will eradicate your descendants:

> I will wipe out all of Ahab's males,
> both slave and free, in Israel;

²² I will make your house like the house of Jeroboam son of Nebat and like the house of Baasha son of Ahijah, because you have angered me and caused Israel to sin.' ²³ The LORD also speaks of Jezebel: 'The dogs will eat Jezebel in the plot of land at Jezreel:

> ²⁴ Anyone who belongs to Ahab and dies in the city,
> the dogs will eat,
> and anyone who dies in the field, the birds will eat.'"

²⁵ Still, there was no one like Ahab, who devoted himself to do what was evil in the LORD's sight, because his wife Jezebel incited him. ²⁶ He committed the most detestable acts by following idols as the Amorites had, whom the LORD had dispossessed before the Israelites.

²⁷ When Ahab heard these words, he tore his clothes, put sackcloth over his body, and fasted. He lay down in sackcloth and walked around subdued. ²⁸ Then the word of the LORD came to Elijah the Tishbite: ²⁹ "Have you seen how Ahab has humbled himself before me? I will not bring the disaster during his lifetime, because he has humbled himself before me. I will bring the disaster on his house during his son's lifetime."

MATTHEW 7:15–20

¹⁵ "Be on your guard against false prophets who come to you in sheep's clothing but inwardly are ravaging wolves. ¹⁶ You'll recognize them by their fruit. Are grapes gathered from thornbushes or figs from thistles? ¹⁷ In the same way, every good tree produces good fruit, but a bad tree produces bad fruit. ¹⁸ A good tree can't produce bad fruit; neither can a bad tree produce good fruit. ¹⁹ Every tree that doesn't produce good fruit is cut down and thrown into the fire. ²⁰ So you'll recognize them by their fruit."

1 Summarize the events of
this story.

2 What stood out to you?
What questions do you have?

3 What is God teaching you
in the reading?

Elijah

The Prophet Who Held Back Rain and Called Down Fire

1 KINGS 18

ELIJAH'S MESSAGE TO AHAB

¹ After a long time, the word of the Lord came to Elijah in the third year: "Go and present yourself to Ahab. I will send rain on the surface of the land." ² So Elijah went to present himself to Ahab.

The famine was severe in Samaria. ³ Ahab called for Obadiah, who was in charge of the palace. Obadiah was a man who greatly feared the Lord ⁴ and took a hundred prophets and hid them, fifty men to a cave, and provided them with food and water when Jezebel slaughtered the Lord's prophets. ⁵ Ahab said to Obadiah, "Go throughout the land to every spring and to every wadi. Perhaps we'll find grass so we can keep the horses and mules alive and not have to destroy any cattle." ⁶ They divided the land between them in order to cover it. Ahab went one way by himself, and Obadiah went the other way by himself.

⁷ While Obadiah was walking along the road, Elijah suddenly met him. When Obadiah recognized him, he fell facedown and said, "Is it you, my lord Elijah?"

⁸ "It is I," he replied. "Go tell your lord, 'Elijah is here!'"

⁹ But Obadiah said, "What sin have I committed, that you are handing your servant over to Ahab to put me to death? ¹⁰ As the Lord your God lives, there is no nation or kingdom where my lord has not sent someone to search for you. When they said, 'He is not here,' he made that kingdom or nation swear they had not found you.

¹¹ "Now you say, 'Go tell your lord, "Elijah is here!"' ¹² But when I leave you, the Spirit of the Lord may carry you off to some place I don't know. Then when I go report to Ahab and he doesn't find you, he will kill me. But I, your servant, have feared the Lord from my youth. ¹³ Wasn't it reported to my lord what I did when

Jezebel slaughtered the LORD's prophets? I hid a hundred of the prophets of the LORD fifty men to a cave, and I provided them with food and water. ¹⁴ Now you say, 'Go tell your lord, "Elijah is here!"' He will kill me!"

¹⁵ Then Elijah said, "As the LORD of Armies lives, in whose presence I stand, today I will present myself to Ahab."

¹⁶ Obadiah went to meet Ahab and told him. Then Ahab went to meet Elijah. ¹⁷ When Ahab saw Elijah, Ahab said to him, "Is that you, the one ruining Israel?"

¹⁸ He replied, "I have not ruined Israel, but you and your father's family have, because you have abandoned the LORD's commands and followed the Baals. ¹⁹ Now summon all Israel to meet me at Mount Carmel, along with the 450 prophets of Baal and the 400 prophets of Asherah who eat at Jezebel's table."

ELIJAH AT MOUNT CARMEL

²⁰ So Ahab summoned all the Israelites and gathered the prophets at Mount Carmel. ²¹ Then Elijah approached all the people and said, "How long will you waver between two opinions? If the LORD is God, follow him. But if Baal, follow him." But the people didn't answer him a word.

²² Then Elijah said to the people, "I am the only remaining prophet of the LORD, but Baal's prophets are 450 men. ²³ Let two bulls be given to us. They are to choose one bull for themselves, cut it in pieces, and place it on the wood but not light the fire. I will prepare the other bull and place it on the wood but not light the fire. ²⁴ Then you call on the name of your god, and I will call on the name of the LORD. The God who answers with fire, he is God."

All the people answered, "That's fine."

²⁵ Then Elijah said to the prophets of Baal, "Since you are so numerous, choose for yourselves one bull and prepare it first. Then call on the name of your god but don't light the fire."

²⁶ So they took the bull that he gave them, prepared it, and called on the name of Baal from morning until noon, saying, "Baal, answer us!" But there was no sound; no one answered. Then they danced around the altar they had made.

²⁷ At noon Elijah mocked them. He said, "Shout loudly, for he's a god! Maybe he's thinking it over; maybe he has wandered away; or maybe he's on the road. Perhaps he's sleeping and will wake up!" ²⁸ They shouted loudly, and cut themselves with knives and spears, according to their custom, until blood gushed over them. ²⁹ All afternoon they kept on raving until the offering of the evening sacrifice, but there was no sound; no one answered, no one paid attention.

³⁰ Then Elijah said to all the people, "Come near me." So all the people approached him. Then he repaired the LORD's altar that had been torn down: ³¹ Elijah took twelve stones—according to the number of the tribes of the sons of Jacob, to whom the word of the LORD had come, saying, "Israel will be your name"— ³² and he built an altar with the stones in the name of the LORD. Then he made a trench around the altar large enough to hold about four gallons. ³³ Next, he arranged the wood, cut up the bull, and placed it on the wood. He said, "Fill four water pots with water and pour it on the offering to be burned and on the wood." ³⁴ Then he said, "A second time!" and they did it a second time. And then he said, "A third time!" and they did it a third time. ³⁵ So the water ran all around the altar; he even filled the trench with water.

³⁶ At the time for offering the evening sacrifice, the prophet Elijah approached the altar and said, "LORD, the God of Abraham, Isaac, and Israel, today let it be known that you are God in Israel and I am your servant, and that at your word I have done all these things. ³⁷ Answer me, LORD! Answer me so that this people will know that you, the LORD, are God and that you have turned their hearts back."

³⁸ Then the LORD's fire fell and consumed the burnt offering, the wood, the stones, and the dust, and it licked up the water that was in the trench. ³⁹ When all the people saw it, they fell facedown and said, "The LORD, he is God! The LORD, he is God!"

⁴⁰ Then Elijah ordered them, "Seize the prophets of Baal! Do not let even one of them escape." So they seized them, and Elijah brought them down to the Wadi Kishon and slaughtered them there. ⁴¹ Elijah said to Ahab, "Go up, eat and drink, for there is the sound of a rainstorm."

⁴² So Ahab went to eat and drink, but Elijah went up to the summit of Carmel. He bent down on the ground and put his face between his knees. ⁴³ Then he said to his servant, "Go up and look toward the sea."

So he went up, looked, and said, "There's nothing."

Seven times Elijah said, "Go back."

⁴⁴ On the seventh time, he reported, "There's a cloud as small as a man's hand coming up from the sea."

Then Elijah said, "Go and tell Ahab, 'Get your chariot ready and go down so the rain doesn't stop you.'"

⁴⁵ In a little while, the sky grew dark with clouds and wind, and there was a downpour. So Ahab got in his chariot and went to Jezreel. ⁴⁶ The power of the LORD was on Elijah, and he tucked his mantle under his belt and ran ahead of Ahab to the entrance of Jezreel.

PROVERBS 20:22

Don't say, "I will avenge this evil!"
Wait on the LORD, and he will rescue you.

RESPONSE

1 Summarize the events of
  this story.

2 What stood out to you?
  What questions do you have?

3 What is God teaching you
  in the reading?

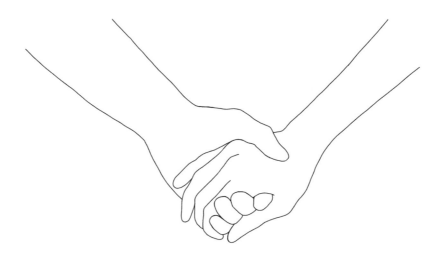

Hosea and Gomer

A Living Prophecy About God's Love for His People

² When the LORD first spoke to Hosea, he said this to him:

> Go and marry a woman of promiscuity,
> and have children of promiscuity,
> for the land is committing blatant acts of promiscuity
> by abandoning the LORD.

³ So he went and married Gomer daughter of Diblaim, and she conceived and bore him a son. ⁴ Then the LORD said to him:

> Name him Jezreel, for in a little while
> I will bring the bloodshed of Jezreel
> on the house of Jehu
> and put an end to the kingdom of the house of Israel.
> ⁵ On that day I will break the bow of Israel
> in the Valley of Jezreel.

⁶ She conceived again and gave birth to a daughter, and the LORD said to him:

> Name her Lo-ruhamah,
> for I will no longer have compassion
> on the house of Israel.
> I will certainly take them away.
> ⁷ But I will have compassion on the house of Judah,
> and I will deliver them by the LORD their God.
> I will not deliver them by bow, sword, or war,
> or by horses and cavalry.

⁸ After Gomer had weaned Lo-ruhamah, she conceived and gave birth to a son. ⁹ Then the LORD said:

> Name him Lo-ammi,
> for you are not my people,
> and I will not be your God.
> ¹⁰ Yet the number of the Israelites
> will be like the sand of the sea,
> which cannot be measured or counted.
> And in the place where they were told:
> You are not my people,
> they will be called: Sons of the living God.

> ¹¹ And the Judeans and the Israelites
> will be gathered together.
> They will appoint for themselves a single ruler
> and go up from the land.
> For the day of Jezreel will be great.

> ¹ Call your brothers: My People
> and your sisters: Compassion.

> …

> ⁵ Yes, their mother is promiscuous;
> she conceived them and acted shamefully.
> For she thought, "I will follow my lovers,
> the men who give me my food and water,
> my wool and flax, my oil and drink."
> ⁶ Therefore, this is what I will do:
> I will block her way with thorns;
> I will enclose her with a wall,
> so that she cannot find her paths.
> ⁷ She will pursue her lovers but not catch them;
> she will look for them but not find them.
> Then she will think,
> "I will go back to my former husband,
> for then it was better for me than now."
> ⁸ She does not recognize
> that it is I who gave her the grain,
> the new wine, and the fresh oil.
> I lavished silver and gold on her,
> which they used for Baal.
> ⁹ Therefore, I will take back my grain in its time
> and my new wine in its season;
> I will take away my wool and linen,
> which were to cover her nakedness.
> ¹⁰ Now I will expose her shame
> in the sight of her lovers,
> and no one will rescue her from my power.
> ¹¹ I will put an end to all her celebrations:
> her feasts, New Moons, and Sabbaths—
> all her festivals.
> ¹² I will devastate her vines and fig trees.

She thinks that these are her wages
that her lovers have given her.
I will turn them into a thicket,
and the wild animals will eat them.
[13] And I will punish her for the days of the Baals,
to which she burned incense.
She put on her rings and her jewelry
and followed her lovers,
but she forgot me.

This is the LORD's declaration.

ISRAEL'S ADULTERY FORGIVEN

[14] Therefore, I am going to persuade her,
lead her to the wilderness,
and speak tenderly to her.
[15] There I will give her vineyards back to her
and make the Valley of Achor
into a gateway of hope.
There she will respond as she did
in the days of her youth,
as in the day she came out of the land of Egypt.
[16] In that day—
this is the LORD's declaration—
you will call me, "My husband,"
and no longer call me, "My Baal."
[17] For I will remove the names of the Baals
from her mouth;
they will no longer be remembered by their names.
[18] On that day I will make a covenant for them
with the wild animals, the birds of the sky,
and the creatures that crawl on the ground.
I will shatter bow, sword,
and weapons of war in the land
and will enable the people to rest securely.
[19] I will take you to be my wife forever.
I will take you to be my wife in righteousness,
justice, love, and compassion.
[20] I will take you to be my wife in faithfulness,
and you will know the LORD.
[21] On that day I will respond—
this is the LORD's declaration.

I will respond to the sky,
and it will respond to the earth.
[22] The earth will respond to the grain,
the new wine, and the fresh oil,
and they will respond to Jezreel.
[23] I will sow her in the land for myself,
and I will have compassion
on Lo-ruhamah;
I will say to Lo-ammi:
You are my people,
and he will say, "You are my God."

HOSEA 3:1–5
WAITING FOR RESTORATION

[1] Then the LORD said to me, "Go again; show love to a woman who is loved by another man and is an adulteress, just as the LORD loves the Israelites though they turn to other gods and love raisin cakes."

[2] So I bought her for fifteen shekels of silver and five bushels of barley. [3] I said to her, "You are to live with me many days. You must not be promiscuous or belong to any man, and I will act the same way toward you."

[4] For the Israelites must live many days without king or prince, without sacrifice or sacred pillar, and without ephod or household idols. [5] Afterward, the people of Israel will return and seek the LORD their God and David their king. They will come with awe to the LORD and to his goodness in the last days.

PSALM 144:2

He is my faithful love and my fortress,
my stronghold and my deliverer.
He is my shield, and I take refuge in him;
he subdues my people under me.

1   Summarize the events of
    this story.

2   What stood out to you?
    What questions do you have?

3   What is God teaching you
    in the reading?

Roasted Strawberry Honey Ice Cream

PREP TIME	WAIT TIME	COOK TIME	SERVINGS
20 minutes	3 hours	30 minutes	8

TORI DIBARTOLOMEO
@tosaltandsee

INGREDIENTS

16 ounces fresh strawberries

2 tablespoons balsamic vinegar

1 tablespoon honey

1 cup whole milk

½ cup sugar

Pinch of salt

2 cups heavy cream

1 teaspoon vanilla

INSTRUCTIONS

Preheat oven to 375°F. Line a rimmed baking sheet with parchment paper and set aside.

Wash, hull, and cut the strawberries into quarters. In a medium bowl, toss the strawberries with balsamic vinegar and honey. Transfer to the pre-lined baking sheet in a single layer. Bake 30 minutes until the juices have thickened.

Once the strawberries have cooled, briefly puree in a blender, allowing small bits of strawberry to remain.

In a small saucepan over low heat, whisk together milk, sugar, and salt until the sugar has dissolved. Remove from heat, and transfer to a large bowl. Stir in the heavy cream and vanilla. Stir in the strawberry puree.

Cover the bowl with plastic wrap. Refrigerate 2 to 3 hours, or overnight.

Pour cooled mixture into an ice cream maker, and churn per manufacturer's instructions. Store in the freezer in an airtight container.

For easy serving, allow ice cream to soften slightly by setting it out at room temperature for 5 minutes. Run the ice cream scoop under hot water before using. This will help to create that perfect scoop of ice cream!

Grace Day

Use this day to pray, rest, and reflect on this week's reading,
giving thanks for the grace that is ours in Christ.

JAMES 3:17

But the wisdom from above is first pure, then peace-loving, gentle, compliant, full of mercy and good fruits, unwavering, without pretense.

Scripture is God-breathed and true. When we memorize it, we carry the gospel with us wherever we go.

This week we'll memorize a verse from Solomon's prayer at the dedication of the temple in Jerusalem on day 44.

Weekly Truth

1 KINGS 8:60

May all the peoples of the earth know that the LORD is God. There is no other!

Find the corresponding memory card in the back of this book.

Hezekiah

The King Who Prayed and Was Twice Rescued

SENNACHERIB'S DEPARTING THREAT

⁸ When the royal spokesman heard that the king of Assyria had pulled out of Lachish, he left and found him fighting against Libnah. ⁹ The king had heard concerning King Tirhakah of Cush, "Look, he has set out to fight against you." So he again sent messengers to Hezekiah, saying, ¹⁰ "Say this to King Hezekiah of Judah: 'Don't let your God, on whom you rely, deceive you by promising that Jerusalem will not be handed over to the king of Assyria. ¹¹ Look, you have heard what the kings of Assyria have done to all the countries: They completely destroyed them. Will you be rescued? ¹² Did the gods of the nations that my predecessors destroyed rescue them—nations such as Gozan, Haran, Rezeph, and the Edenites in Telassar? ¹³ Where is the king of Hamath, the king of Arpad, the king of the city of Sepharvaim, Hena, or Ivvah?'"

HEZEKIAH'S PRAYER

¹⁴ Hezekiah took the letter from the messengers' hands, read it, then went up to the LORD's temple, and spread it out before the LORD. ¹⁵ Then Hezekiah prayed before the LORD:

LORD God of Israel, enthroned between the cherubim, you are God—you alone—of all the kingdoms of the earth. You made the heavens and the earth. ¹⁶ Listen closely, LORD, and hear; open your eyes, LORD, and see. Hear the words that Sennacherib has sent to mock the living God. ¹⁷ LORD, it is true that the kings of Assyria have devastated the nations and their lands. ¹⁸ They have thrown their gods into the fire, for they were not gods but made by human hands—wood and stone. So they have destroyed them. ¹⁹ Now, LORD our God, please save us from his power so that all the kingdoms of the earth may know that you, LORD, are God—you alone.

...

DEFEAT AND DEATH OF SENNACHERIB

³⁵ That night the angel of the LORD went out and struck down one hundred eighty-five thousand in the camp of the Assyrians. When the people got up the next morning—there were all the dead bodies! ³⁶ So King Sennacherib of Assyria broke camp and left. He returned home and lived in Nineveh.

³⁷ One day, while he was worshiping in the temple of his god Nisroch, his sons Adrammelech and Sharezer struck him down with the sword and escaped to the land of Ararat. Then his son Esar-haddon became king in his place.

HEZEKIAH'S ILLNESS AND RECOVERY

¹ In those days Hezekiah became terminally ill. The prophet Isaiah son of Amoz came and said to him, "This is what the LORD says: 'Set your house in order, for you are about to die; you will not recover.'"

² Then Hezekiah turned his face to the wall and prayed to the LORD. ³ He said, "Please, LORD, remember how I have walked before you faithfully and wholeheartedly, and have done what pleases you." And Hezekiah wept bitterly.

⁴ Then the word of the LORD came to Isaiah: ⁵ "Go and tell Hezekiah, 'This is what the LORD God of your ancestor David says: I have heard your prayer; I have seen your tears. Look, I am going to add fifteen years to your life. ⁶ And I will rescue you and this city from the grasp of the king of Assyria; I will defend this city. ⁷ This is the sign to you from the LORD that he will do what he has promised: ⁸ I am going to make the sun's shadow that goes down on the stairway of Ahaz go back by ten steps.'" So the sun's shadow went back the ten steps it had descended.

⁹ A poem by King Hezekiah of Judah after he had been sick and had recovered from his illness:

¹⁰ I said: In the prime of my life
I must go to the gates of Sheol;
I am deprived of the rest of my years.
¹¹ I said: I will never see the LORD,
the LORD in the land of the living;
I will not look on humanity any longer
with the inhabitants of what is passing away.
¹² My dwelling is plucked up and removed from me
like a shepherd's tent.

LORD God of Israel, enthroned between the cherubim, you are God—you alone—of all the kingdoms of the earth. You made the heavens and the earth.

I have rolled up my life like a weaver;
he cuts me off from the loom.
By nightfall you make an end of me.
[13] I thought until the morning:
He will break all my bones like a lion.
By nightfall you make an end of me.
[14] I chirp like a swallow or a crane;
I moan like a dove.
My eyes grow weak looking upward.
Lord, I am oppressed; support me.

[15] What can I say?
He has spoken to me,
and he himself has done it.
I walk along slowly all my years
because of the bitterness of my soul.
[16] Lord, by such things people live,
and in every one of them my spirit finds life;

you have restored me to health
and let me live.
[17] Indeed, it was for my own well-being
that I had such intense bitterness;
but your love has delivered me
from the Pit of destruction,
for you have thrown all my sins behind your back.
[18] For Sheol cannot thank you;
Death cannot praise you.
Those who go down to the Pit
cannot hope for your faithfulness.
[19] The living, only the living can thank you,
as I do today;
a father will make your faithfulness known to children.
[20] The LORD is ready to save me;
we will play stringed instruments
all the days of our lives
at the house of the LORD.

1 Summarize the events of
this story.

2 What stood out to you?
What questions do you have?

3 What is God teaching you
in the reading?

Ezekiel

A Prophetic Voice in Exile

EZEKIEL 2

MISSION TO REBELLIOUS ISRAEL

¹ He said to me, "Son of man, stand up on your feet and I will speak with you." ² As he spoke to me, the Spirit entered me and set me on my feet, and I listened to the one who was speaking to me. ³ He said to me, "Son of man, I am sending you to the Israelites, to the rebellious pagans who have rebelled against me. The Israelites and their ancestors have transgressed against me to this day. ⁴ The descendants are obstinate and hardhearted. I am sending you to them, and you must say to them, 'This is what the Lord God says.' ⁵ Whether they listen or refuse to listen—for they are a rebellious house—they will know that a prophet has been among them.

⁶ "But you, son of man, do not be afraid of them and do not be afraid of their words, even though briers and thorns are beside you and you live among scorpions. Don't be afraid of their words or discouraged by the look on their faces, for they are a rebellious house. ⁷ Speak my words to them whether they listen or refuse to listen, for they are rebellious.

⁸ "And you, son of man, listen to what I tell you: Do not be rebellious like that rebellious house. Open your mouth and eat what I am giving you." ⁹ So I looked and saw a hand reaching out to me, and there was a written scroll in it. ¹⁰ When he unrolled it before me, it was written on the front and back; words of lamentation, mourning, and woe were written on it.

EZEKIEL 3:1–15

¹ He said to me: "Son of man, eat what you find here. Eat this scroll, then go and speak to the house of Israel." ² So I opened my mouth, and he fed me the scroll. ³ "Son of man," he said to me, "feed your stomach and fill your belly with this scroll I am giving you." So I ate it, and it was as sweet as honey in my mouth.

⁴ Then he said to me: "Son of man, go to the house of Israel and speak my words to them. ⁵ For you are not being sent to a people of unintelligible speech or a difficult language but to the house of Israel— ⁶ not to the many peoples of unintelligible speech or a difficult language, whose words you cannot understand. No doubt, if I sent you to them, they would listen to you. ⁷ But the house of Israel will not want to listen to you because they do not want to listen to me. For the whole house of Israel is hardheaded and hardhearted. ⁸ Look, I have made your face as hard as their faces and your forehead as hard as their foreheads. ⁹ I have made your forehead like a diamond, harder than flint. Don't be afraid of them or discouraged by the look on their faces, though they are a rebellious house."

¹⁰ Next he said to me: "Son of man, listen carefully to all my words that I speak to you and take them to heart. ¹¹ Go to your people, the exiles, and speak to them. Tell them, 'This is what the Lord God says,' whether they listen or refuse to listen."

¹² The Spirit then lifted me up, and I heard a loud rumbling sound behind me—bless the glory of the Lord in his place!— ¹³ with the sound of the living creatures' wings brushing against each other and the sound of the wheels beside them, a loud rumbling sound. ¹⁴ The Spirit lifted me up and took me away. I left in bitterness and in an angry spirit, and the Lord's hand was on me powerfully. ¹⁵ I came to the exiles at Tel-abib, who were living by the Chebar Canal, and I sat there among them stunned for seven days.

EZEKIEL 12:1–20
EZEKIEL DRAMATIZES THE EXILE

¹ The word of the Lord came to me: ² "Son of man, you are living among a rebellious house. They have eyes to see but do not see, and ears to hear but do not hear, for they are a rebellious house.

³ "Now you, son of man, get your bags ready for exile and go into exile in their sight during the day. You will go into exile from your place to another place while they watch; perhaps they will understand, though they are a rebellious house. ⁴ During the day, bring out your bags like an exile's bags while they look on. Then in the evening go out in their sight like those going into exile. ⁵ As they watch, dig through the wall and take the bags out through it. ⁶ And while they look on, lift the bags to your shoulder and take them out in the dark; cover your face so that you cannot see the land. For I have made you a sign to the house of Israel."

⁷ So I did just as I was commanded. In the daytime I brought out my bags like an exile's bags. In the evening I dug through the wall by hand; I took them out in the dark, carrying them on my shoulder in their sight.

⁸ In the morning the word of the Lord came to me: ⁹ "Son of man, hasn't the house of Israel, that rebellious house, asked you, 'What are you doing?' ¹⁰ Say to them, 'This is what the Lord God says: This pronouncement concerns the prince in Jerusalem and the whole house of Israel living there.' ¹¹ You are to say, 'I am a sign for you. Just as I have done, it will be done to them; they will go into exile, into captivity.' ¹² The prince who is among them will lift his bags to his shoulder in the dark and go out. They will dig through the wall to bring him out through it. He will cover his face so he cannot see the land with his eyes. ¹³ But I will spread my net over him, and he will be caught in my snare. I will bring him to Babylon, the land of the Chaldeans, yet he will not see it, and he will die there. ¹⁴ I will also scatter all the attendants who surround him and all his troops to every direction of the wind, and I will draw a sword to chase after them. ¹⁵ They will know that I am the Lord when I disperse them among the nations and scatter them among the countries. ¹⁶ But I will spare a few of them from the sword, famine, and plague, so that among the nations where they go they can tell about all their detestable practices. Then they will know that I am the Lord."

He said to me: "Son of man, eat what you find here. Eat this scroll, then go and speak to the house of Israel."

———

EZEKIEL DRAMATIZES ISRAEL'S ANXIETY

[17] The word of the LORD came to me: [18] "Son of man, eat your bread with trembling and drink your water with anxious shaking. [19] Then say to the people of the land, 'This is what the LORD God says about the residents of Jerusalem in the land of Israel: They will eat their bread with anxiety and drink their water in dread, for their land will be stripped of everything in it because of the violence of all who live there. [20] The inhabited cities will be destroyed, and the land will become dreadful. Then you will know that I am the LORD.'"

ISAIAH 55:6–7

[6] Seek the LORD while he may be found;
call to him while he is near.
[7] Let the wicked one abandon his way
and the sinful one his thoughts;
let him return to the LORD,
so he may have compassion on him,
and to our God, for he will freely forgive.

1 Summarize the events of
   this story.

2 What stood out to you?
   What questions do you have?

3 What is God teaching you
   in the reading?

Daniel

Faithful to God in a Foreign Land

DANIEL 2
NEBUCHADNEZZAR'S DREAM

¹ In the second year of his reign, Nebuchadnezzar had dreams that troubled him, and sleep deserted him. ² So the king gave orders to summon the magicians, mediums, sorcerers, and Chaldeans to tell the king his dreams. When they came and stood before the king, ³ he said to them, "I have had a dream and am anxious to understand it."

⁴ The Chaldeans spoke to the king (Aramaic begins here): "May the king live forever. Tell your servants the dream, and we will give the interpretation."

⁵ The king replied to the Chaldeans, "My word is final: If you don't tell me the dream and its interpretation, you will be torn limb from limb, and your houses will be made a garbage dump. ⁶ But if you make the dream and its interpretation known to me, you'll receive gifts, a reward, and great honor from me. So make the dream and its interpretation known to me."

⁷ They answered a second time, "May the king tell the dream to his servants, and we will make known the interpretation."

⁸ The king replied, "I know for certain you are trying to gain some time, because you see that my word is final. ⁹ If you don't tell me the dream, there is one decree for you. You have conspired to tell me something false or fraudulent until the situation changes. So tell me the dream and I will know you can give me its interpretation."

¹⁰ The Chaldeans answered the king, "No one on earth can make known what the king requests. Consequently, no king, however great and powerful, has ever asked anything like this of any magician, medium, or Chaldean. ¹¹ What the king is asking is so difficult that no one can make it known to him except the gods, whose dwelling is not with mortals." ¹² Because of this, the king became violently angry and gave orders to destroy all the wise men of Babylon. ¹³ The decree was issued that the wise men were to be executed, and they searched for Daniel and his friends, to execute them.

¹⁴ Then Daniel responded with tact and discretion to Arioch, the captain of the king's guard, who had gone out to execute the wise men of Babylon. ¹⁵ He asked Arioch, the king's officer, "Why is the decree from the king so harsh?" Then Arioch explained the situation to Daniel. ¹⁶ So Daniel went and asked the king to give him some time, so that he could give the king the interpretation.

¹⁷ Then Daniel went to his house and told his friends Hananiah, Mishael, and Azariah about the matter, ¹⁸ urging them to ask the God of the heavens for mercy concerning this mystery, so Daniel and his friends would not be destroyed

with the rest of Babylon's wise men. [19] The mystery was then revealed to Daniel in a vision at night, and Daniel praised the God of the heavens [20] and declared:

May the name of God
be praised forever and ever,
for wisdom and power belong to him.
[21] He changes the times and seasons;
he removes kings and establishes kings.
He gives wisdom to the wise
and knowledge to those
who have understanding.
[22] He reveals the deep and hidden things;
he knows what is in the darkness,
and light dwells with him.
[23] I offer thanks and praise to you,
God of my fathers,
because you have given me
wisdom and power.
And now you have let me know
what we asked of you,
for you have let us know
the king's mystery.

[24] Therefore Daniel went to Arioch, whom the king had assigned to destroy the wise men of Babylon. He came and said to him, "Don't destroy the wise men of Babylon! Bring me before the king, and I will give him the interpretation."

[25] Then Arioch quickly brought Daniel before the king and said to him, "I have found a man among the Judean exiles who can let the king know the interpretation."

[26] The king said in reply to Daniel, whose name was Belteshazzar, "Are you able to tell me the dream I had and its interpretation?"

[27] Daniel answered the king: "No wise man, medium, magician, or diviner is able to make known to the king the mystery he asked about. [28] But there is a God in heaven who reveals mysteries, and he has let King Nebuchadnezzar know what will happen in the last days. Your dream and the visions that came into your mind as you lay in bed were these: [29] Your Majesty, while you were in your bed, thoughts came to your mind about what will happen in the future. The revealer of mysteries has let you know what will happen. [30] As for me, this mystery has been revealed to me, not because I have more wisdom than anyone living, but in order that the interpretation might be made known to the king, and that you may understand the thoughts of your mind.

[31] "Your Majesty, as you were watching, suddenly a colossal statue appeared. That statue, tall and dazzling, was standing in front of you, and its appearance was terrifying. [32] The head of the statue was pure gold, its chest and arms were silver, its stomach and thighs were bronze, [33] its legs were iron, and its feet were partly iron and partly fired clay. [34] As you were watching, a stone broke off without a hand touching it, struck the statue on its feet of iron and fired clay, and crushed them. [35] Then the iron, the fired clay, the bronze, the silver, and the gold were shattered and became like chaff from the summer threshing floors. The wind carried them away, and not a trace of them could be found. But the stone that struck the statue became a great mountain and filled the whole earth.

[36] "This was the dream; now we will tell the king its interpretation. [37] Your Majesty, you are king of kings. The God of the heavens has given you sovereignty, power, strength, and glory. [38] Wherever people live—or wild animals, or birds of the sky—he has handed them over to you and made you ruler over them all. You are the head of gold.

[39] "After you, there will arise another kingdom, inferior to yours, and then another, a third kingdom, of bronze, which will rule the whole earth. [40] A fourth kingdom will be as strong as iron; for iron crushes and shatters everything, and like iron that smashes, it will crush and smash all the others. [41] You saw the feet and toes, partly of a potter's fired clay and partly of iron—it will be a divided kingdom, though some of the strength of iron will be in it. You saw the iron mixed with clay, [42] and that the toes of the feet were partly iron and partly fired clay—part of the kingdom will be strong, and part will be brittle. [43] You saw the iron mixed with clay—the peoples will mix with one another but will not hold together, just as iron does not mix with fired clay.

[44] "In the days of those kings, the God of the heavens will set up a kingdom that will never be destroyed, and this kingdom will not be left to another people. It will crush all these kingdoms and bring them to an end, but will itself endure forever. [45] You saw a stone break off from the mountain without a hand touching it, and it crushed the iron, bronze, fired clay, silver, and gold. The great God has told the king what will happen in the future. The dream is certain, and its interpretation reliable."

NEBUCHADNEZZAR'S RESPONSE

[46] Then King Nebuchadnezzar fell facedown, worshiped Daniel, and gave orders to present an offering and incense to him. [47] The king said to Daniel, "Your God is indeed God of gods, Lord of kings, and a revealer of mysteries, since you were able to reveal this mystery." [48] Then the king promoted Daniel and gave him many generous gifts. He made him ruler over the entire province of Babylon and chief governor over all the wise men of Babylon. [49] At Daniel's request, the king appointed Shadrach, Meshach, and Abednego to manage the province of Babylon. But Daniel remained at the king's court.

LUKE 12:11–12

[11] "Whenever they bring you before synagogues and rulers and authorities, don't worry about how you should defend yourselves or what you should say. [12] For the Holy Spirit will teach you at that very hour what must be said."

COLOSSIANS 3:23–24

[23] Whatever you do, do it from the heart, as something done for the Lord and not for people, [24] knowing that you will receive the reward of an inheritance from the Lord. You serve the Lord Christ.

1 Summarize the events of
   this story.

2 What stood out to you?
   What questions do you have?

3 What is God teaching you
   in the reading?

DAY 53
WEEK 8

Shadrach, Meshach, and Abednego

Men of God Who Would Not Compromise

DANIEL 3

NEBUCHADNEZZAR'S GOLD STATUE

[1] King Nebuchadnezzar made a gold statue, ninety feet high and nine feet wide. He set it up on the plain of Dura in the province of Babylon. [2] King Nebuchadnezzar sent word to assemble the satraps, prefects, governors, advisers, treasurers, judges, magistrates, and all the rulers of the provinces to attend the dedication of the statue King Nebuchadnezzar had set up. [3] So the satraps, prefects, governors, advisers, treasurers, judges, magistrates, and all the rulers of the provinces assembled for the dedication of the statue the king had set up. Then they stood before the statue Nebuchadnezzar had set up.

[4] A herald loudly proclaimed, "People of every nation and language, you are commanded: [5] When you hear the sound of the horn, flute, zither, lyre, harp, drum, and every kind of music, you are to fall facedown and worship the gold statue that King Nebuchadnezzar has set up. [6] But whoever does not fall down and worship will immediately be thrown into a furnace of blazing fire."

[7] Therefore, when all the people heard the sound of the horn, flute, zither, lyre, harp, and every kind of music, people of every nation and language fell down and worshiped the gold statue that King Nebuchadnezzar had set up.

THE FURNACE OF BLAZING FIRE

[8] Some Chaldeans took this occasion to come forward and maliciously accuse the Jews. [9] They said to King Nebuchadnezzar, "May the king live forever. [10] You as king

have issued a decree that everyone who hears the sound of the horn, flute, zither, lyre, harp, drum, and every kind of music must fall down and worship the gold statue. [11] Whoever does not fall down and worship will be thrown into a furnace of blazing fire. [12] There are some Jews you have appointed to manage the province of Babylon: Shadrach, Meshach, and Abednego. These men have ignored you, the king; they do not serve your gods or worship the gold statue you have set up."

[13] Then in a furious rage Nebuchadnezzar gave orders to bring in Shadrach, Meshach, and Abednego. So these men were brought before the king. [14] Nebuchadnezzar asked them, "Shadrach, Meshach, and Abednego, is it true that you don't serve my gods or worship the gold statue I have set up? [15] Now if you're ready, when you hear the sound of the horn, flute, zither, lyre, harp, drum, and every kind of music, fall down and worship the statue I made. But if you don't worship it, you will immediately be thrown into a furnace of blazing fire—and who is the god who can rescue you from my power?"

[16] Shadrach, Meshach, and Abednego replied to the king, "Nebuchadnezzar, we don't need to give you an answer to this question. [17] If the God we serve exists, then he can rescue us from the furnace of blazing fire, and he can rescue us from the power of you, the king. [18] But even if he does not rescue us, we want you as king to know that we will not serve your gods or worship the gold statue you set up."

[19] Then Nebuchadnezzar was filled with rage, and the expression on his face changed toward Shadrach, Meshach, and Abednego. He gave orders to heat the furnace seven times more than was customary, [20] and he commanded some of the best soldiers in his army to tie up Shadrach, Meshach, and Abednego and throw them into the furnace of blazing fire. [21] So these men, in their trousers, robes, head coverings, and other clothes, were tied up and thrown into the furnace of blazing fire. [22] Since the king's command was so urgent and the furnace extremely hot, the raging flames killed those men who carried Shadrach, Meshach, and Abednego up. [23] And these three men, Shadrach, Meshach, and Abednego fell, bound, into the furnace of blazing fire.

DELIVERED FROM THE FIRE

[24] Then King Nebuchadnezzar jumped up in alarm. He said to his advisers, "Didn't we throw three men, bound, into the fire?"

"Yes, of course, Your Majesty," they replied to the king.

[25] He exclaimed, "Look! I see four men, not tied, walking around in the fire unharmed; and the fourth looks like a son of the gods."

[26] Nebuchadnezzar then approached the door of the furnace of blazing fire and called: "Shadrach, Meshach, and Abednego, you servants of the Most High God—

"You will not be scorched when you walk through the fire, and the flame will not burn you."

come out!" So Shadrach, Meshach, and Abednego came out of the fire. [27] When the satraps, prefects, governors, and the king's advisers gathered around, they saw that the fire had no effect on the bodies of these men: not a hair of their heads was singed, their robes were unaffected, and there was no smell of fire on them. [28] Nebuchadnezzar exclaimed, "Praise to the God of Shadrach, Meshach, and Abednego! He sent his angel and rescued his servants who trusted in him. They violated the king's command and risked their lives rather than serve or worship any god except their own God. [29] Therefore I issue a decree that anyone of any people, nation, or language who says anything offensive against the God of Shadrach, Meshach, and Abednego will be torn limb from limb and his house made a garbage dump. For there is no other god who is able to deliver like this." [30] Then the king rewarded Shadrach, Meshach, and Abednego in the province of Babylon.

ISAIAH 43:2

"I will be with you
when you pass through the waters,
and when you pass through the rivers,
they will not overwhelm you.
You will not be scorched
when you walk through the fire,
and the flame will not burn you."

1 Summarize the events of
   this story.

2 What stood out to you?
   What questions do you have?

3 What is God teaching you
   in the reading?

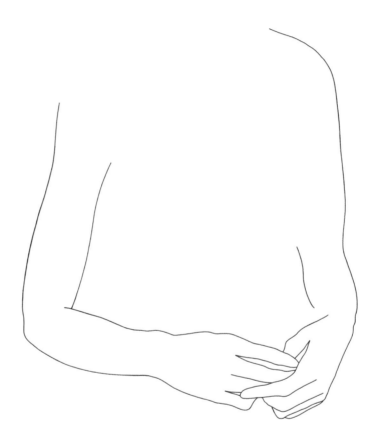

Esther

Queen for Such a Time As This

THE SEARCH FOR A NEW QUEEN

[1] Some time later, when King Ahasuerus's rage had cooled down, he remembered Vashti, what she had done, and what was decided against her. [2] The king's personal attendants suggested, "Let a search be made for beautiful young virgins for the king. [3] Let the king appoint commissioners in each province of his kingdom, so that they may gather all the beautiful young virgins to the harem at the fortress of Susa. Put them under the supervision of Hegai, the king's eunuch, keeper of the women, and give them the required beauty treatments. [4] Then the young woman who pleases the king will become queen instead of Vashti." This suggestion pleased the king, and he did accordingly.

[5] In the fortress of Susa, there was a Jewish man named Mordecai son of Jair, son of Shimei, son of Kish, a Benjaminite. [6] He had been taken into exile from Jerusalem with the other captives when King Nebuchadnezzar of Babylon took King Jeconiah of Judah into exile. [7] Mordecai was the legal guardian of his cousin Hadassah (that is, Esther), because she had no father or mother. The young woman had a beautiful figure and was extremely good-looking. When her father and mother died, Mordecai had adopted her as his own daughter.

[8] When the king's command and edict became public knowledge and when many young women were gathered at the fortress of Susa under Hegai's supervision, Esther was taken to the palace, into the supervision of Hegai, keeper of the women. [9] The young woman pleased him and gained his favor so that he accelerated the process of the beauty treatments and the special diet that she received. He assigned seven hand-picked female servants to her from the palace and transferred her and her servants to the harem's best quarters.

[10] Esther did not reveal her ethnicity or her family background, because Mordecai had ordered her not to make them known. [11] Every day Mordecai took a walk in front of the harem's courtyard to learn how Esther was doing and to see what was happening to her.

[12] During the year before each young woman's turn to go to King Ahasuerus, the harem regulation required her to receive beauty treatments with oil of myrrh for six months and then with perfumes and cosmetics for another six months. [13] When the young woman would go to the king, she was given whatever she requested to take with her from the harem to the palace. [14] She would go in the evening, and in the morning she would return to a second harem under the supervision of the king's eunuch Shaashgaz, keeper of the concubines. She never went to the king again, unless he desired her and summoned her by name.

Who knows, perhaps you have come to your royal position for such a time as this.

ESTHER BECOMES QUEEN

[15] Esther was the daughter of Abihail, the uncle of Mordecai who had adopted her as his own daughter. When her turn came to go to the king, she did not ask for anything except what Hegai, the king's eunuch, keeper of the women, suggested. Esther gained favor in the eyes of everyone who saw her.

[16] She was taken to King Ahasuerus in the palace in the tenth month, the month Tebeth, in the seventh year of his reign. [17] The king loved Esther more than all the other women. She won more favor and approval from him than did any of the other virgins. He placed the royal crown on her head and made her queen in place of Vashti. [18] The king held a great banquet for all his officials and staff. It was Esther's banquet. He freed his provinces from tax payments and gave gifts worthy of the king's bounty.

ESTHER 3:1-6
HAMAN'S PLAN TO KILL THE JEWS

[1] After all this took place, King Ahasuerus honored Haman, son of Hammedatha the Agagite. He promoted him in rank and gave him a higher position than all the other officials. [2] The entire royal staff at the King's Gate bowed down and paid homage to Haman, because the king had commanded this to be done for him. But Mordecai would not bow down or pay homage. [3] The members of the royal staff at the King's Gate asked Mordecai, "Why are you disobeying the king's command?" [4] When they had warned him day after day and he still would not listen to them, they told Haman in order to see if Mordecai's actions would be tolerated, since he had told them he was a Jew.

[5] When Haman saw that Mordecai was not bowing down or paying him homage, he was filled with rage. [6] And when he learned of Mordecai's ethnic identity, it seemed repugnant to Haman to do away with Mordecai alone. He planned to destroy all of Mordecai's people, the Jews, throughout Ahasuerus's kingdom.

ESTHER 4
MORDECAI APPEALS TO ESTHER

[1] When Mordecai learned all that had occurred, he tore his clothes, put on sackcloth and ashes, went into the middle of the city, and cried loudly and bitterly. [2] He went only as far as the King's Gate, since the law prohibited anyone wearing sackcloth from entering the King's Gate. [3] There was great mourning among the Jewish people in every province where the king's command and edict came. They fasted, wept, and lamented, and many lay in sackcloth and ashes.

[4] Esther's female servants and her eunuchs came and reported the news to her, and the queen was overcome with fear. She sent clothes for Mordecai to wear so that he would take off his sackcloth, but he did not accept them. [5] Esther summoned Hathach, one of the king's eunuchs who attended her, and dispatched him to Mordecai to learn what

he was doing and why. [6] So Hathach went out to Mordecai in the city square in front of the King's Gate. [7] Mordecai told him everything that had happened as well as the exact amount of money Haman had promised to pay the royal treasury for the slaughter of the Jews.

[8] Mordecai also gave him a copy of the written decree issued in Susa ordering their destruction, so that Hathach might show it to Esther, explain it to her, and command her to approach the king, implore his favor, and plead with him personally for her people. [9] Hathach came and repeated Mordecai's response to Esther.

[10] Esther spoke to Hathach and commanded him to tell Mordecai, [11] "All the royal officials and the people of the royal provinces know that one law applies to every man or woman who approaches the king in the inner courtyard and who has not been summoned—the death penalty— unless the king extends the gold scepter, allowing that person to live. I have not been summoned to appear before the king for the last thirty days." [12] Esther's response was reported to Mordecai.

[13] Mordecai told the messenger to reply to Esther, "Don't think that you will escape the fate of all the Jews because you are in the king's palace. [14] If you keep silent at this time, relief and deliverance will come to the Jewish people from another place, but you and your father's family will be destroyed. Who knows, perhaps you have come to your royal position for such a time as this."

[15] Esther sent this reply to Mordecai: [16] "Go and assemble all the Jews who can be found in Susa and fast for me. Don't eat or drink for three days, night or day. I and my female servants will also fast in the same way. After that, I will go to the king even if it is against the law. If I perish, I perish." [17] So Mordecai went and did everything Esther had commanded him.

ESTHER 8:1–7
ESTHER INTERVENES FOR THE JEWS

[1] That same day King Ahasuerus awarded Queen Esther the estate of Haman, the enemy of the Jews. Mordecai entered the king's presence because Esther had revealed her relationship to Mordecai. [2] The king removed his signet ring he had recovered from Haman and gave it to Mordecai, and Esther put him in charge of Haman's estate.

[3] Then Esther addressed the king again. She fell at his feet, wept, and begged him to revoke the evil of Haman the Agagite and his plot he had devised against the Jews. [4] The king extended the gold scepter toward Esther, so she got up and stood before the king.

[5] She said, "If it pleases the king and I have found favor before him, if the matter seems right to the king and I am pleasing in his eyes, let a royal edict be written. Let it revoke the documents the scheming Haman son of Hammedatha the Agagite wrote to destroy the Jews who are in all the king's provinces. [6] For how could I bear to see the disaster that would come on my people? How could I bear to see the destruction of my relatives?"

[7] King Ahasuerus said to Esther the queen and to Mordecai the Jew, "Look, I have given Haman's estate to Esther, and he was hanged on the gallows because he attacked the Jews."

HEBREWS 4:14–16
OUR GREAT HIGH PRIEST

[14] Therefore, since we have a great high priest who has passed through the heavens—Jesus the Son of God—let us hold fast to our confession. [15] For we do not have a high priest who is unable to sympathize with our weaknesses, but one who has been tempted in every way as we are, yet without sin. [16] Therefore, let us approach the throne of grace with boldness, so that we may receive mercy and find grace to help us in time of need.

1   Summarize the events of
this story.

2   What stood out to you?
What questions do you have?

3   What is God teaching you
in the reading?

Peach Raspberry Galette

PREP TIME	WAIT TIME	BAKE TIME	SERVINGS
40 minutes	60 minutes	60 minutes	8

TORI DIBARTOLOMEO

@tosaltandsee

A NOTE FROM TORI

You can make the dough with a food processor instead. Pulse the flour and salt together briefly. Add the butter and pulse until it resembles coarse, pea-sized crumbs. With the processor running, add the ice cold water until it all comes together. Resume the original recipe at step #3.

INGREDIENTS

1 ¼ cups flour

½ teaspoon salt

1 stick unsalted butter, cold and cubed

6 tablespoons ice–cold water

3 peaches, thinly sliced

6 ounces raspberries

⅓ cup sugar

1 tablespoon + 1 teaspoon cornstarch

1 teaspoon lemon juice

¼ teaspoon cardamon

1 tablespoon heavy cream

Turbinado sugar

Vanilla ice cream, optional

INSTRUCTIONS

Sift together flour and salt into a medium bowl. Using a pastry blender, cut in the butter until the mixture resembles coarse, pea-sized crumbs.

Add ice water until the dough sticks together when squeezed with your fingers. The dough will look shaggy at this point.

Turn the dough out onto a lightly floured surface. Work into a ball, then flatten into a thick disk.

Wrap dough in plastic wrap. Refrigerate at least 1 hour.

Preheat oven to 400°F. Line a baking sheet with parchment paper and set aside.

For the filling, place the peach slices and raspberries in a large bowl. Add sugar, cornstarch, lemon juice, and cardamon. Gently toss the fruit until well coated.

Roll the dough into a 12-inch circle on a lightly floured surface. Transfer to the prepared baking sheet.

Arrange fruit mixture on the dough, leaving a 1 ½-inch border. Gently fold the border over the fruit, pinching the dough together.

Brush the edges of the dough with cream, and sprinkle with sugar. Bake 50 to 60 minutes, until the edges are golden and the filling is bubbling slightly.

Serve with vanilla ice cream.

Grace Day

DAY 55
WEEK 8

Use this day to pray, rest, and reflect on this week's reading,
giving thanks for the grace that is ours in Christ.

COLOSSIANS 3:23–24

Whatever you do, do it from the heart, as something done for the Lord and not for people, knowing that you will receive the reward of an inheritance from the Lord. You serve the Lord Christ.

Scripture is God-breathed and true. When we memorize it, we carry the gospel with us wherever we go.

This week we'll memorize a reminder from the prophet Daniel, whose story we read on day 52, about our great God who holds the course of history in His hands.

Weekly Truth

DANIEL 2:21

He changes the times and seasons;
he removes kings and establishes kings.
He gives wisdom to the wise
and knowledge to those
who have understanding.

Find the corresponding memory card in the back of this book.

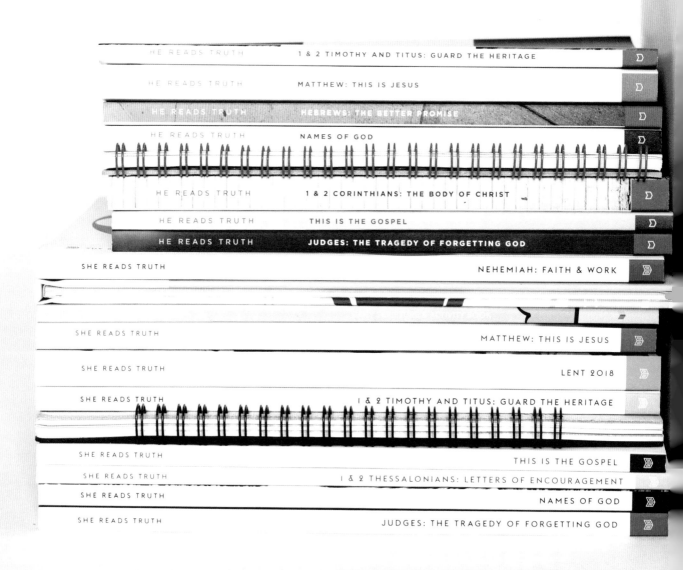

HE READS TRUTH   1 & 2 TIMOTHY AND TITUS: GUARD THE HERITAGE   Σ

HE READS TRUTH   MATTHEW: THIS IS JESUS   Σ

HE READS TRUTH   HEBREWS: THE BETTER PROMISE   Σ

HE READS TRUTH   NAMES OF GOD   Σ

HE READS TRUTH   1 & 2 CORINTHIANS: THE BODY OF CHRIST   Σ

HE READS TRUTH   THIS IS THE GOSPEL   Σ

HE READS TRUTH   JUDGES: THE TRAGEDY OF FORGETTING GOD   Σ

SHE READS TRUTH   NEHEMIAH: FAITH & WORK   ⟫

SHE READS TRUTH   MATTHEW: THIS IS JESUS   ⟫

SHE READS TRUTH   LENT 2018   ⟫

SHE READS TRUTH   1 & 2 TIMOTHY AND TITUS: GUARD THE HERITAGE   ⟫

SHE READS TRUTH   THIS IS THE GOSPEL   ⟫

SHE READS TRUTH   1 & 2 THESSALONIANS: LETTERS OF ENCOURAGEMENT

SHE READS TRUTH   NAMES OF GOD   ⟫

SHE READS TRUTH   JUDGES: THE TRAGEDY OF FORGETTING GOD   ⟫

"WHERE DO I START?"

It's one of the most challenging parts of reading the Bible: knowing where to begin. She Reads Truth Auto-Ship gives you the direction and accountability you need to make daily Scripture reading a reality.

As an Auto-Ship subscriber, you'll receive a new Study Book each month that will guide you through God's Word. With helpful learning tools and thoughtful design, these beautiful books provide a daily framework for reading and understanding Scripture.

Sign up today to start your journey to becoming a woman in the Word of God every day.

AUTOSHIP.SHOPSHEREADSTRUTH.COM

DOWNLOAD THE APP

STOP BY
shereadstruth.com

SHOP
shopshereadstruth.com

SEND A NOTE
hello@shereadstruth.com

SHARE
#SheReadsTruth

SHE READS TRUTH *is a worldwide community of women who read God's Word together every day.*

Founded in 2012, She Reads Truth invites women of all ages to engage with Scripture through daily reading plans, online conversation led by a vibrant community of contributors, and offline resources created at the intersection of beauty, goodness, and Truth.

FOR THE RECORD

WHERE DID I STUDY?

O HOME
O OFFICE
O COFFEE SHOP
O CHURCH
O A FRIEND'S HOUSE
O OTHER

WHAT WAS I LISTENING TO?

ARTIST:

SONG:

PLAYLIST:

WHEN DID I STUDY?

MORNING

AFTERNOON

NIGHT

What did I learn?

WHAT WAS HAPPENING IN MY LIFE?

WHAT WAS HAPPENING IN THE WORLD?

MONTH	DAY	YEAR

END DATE